SHOWERS
of
BLESSINGS

The Beatitudes

MAX W. JACKSON

ISBN 978-1-0980-4375-9 (paperback)
ISBN 978-1-0980-4376-6 (digital)

Copyright © 2020 by Max W. Jackson

All rights reserved. No part of this publication may be reproduced, distributed, or transmitted in any form or by any means, including photocopying, recording, or other electronic or mechanical methods without the prior written permission of the publisher. For permission requests, solicit the publisher via the address below.

Christian Faith Publishing, Inc.
832 Park Avenue
Meadville, PA 16335
www.christianfaithpublishing.com

Printed in the United States of America

In memory of Lorenzo Pryor

Now it shall come to pass, if you "diligently obey" the
voice of the LORD your God, to observe carefully all His
commandments which I command you today, blessed shall you
be. And all these blessings shall come upon you and overtake
you, because you obey the voice of the LORD your God:
Blessed shall you be in the city, and blessed
shall you be in the country.
Blessed shall be the fruit of your body, the produce of
your ground and the increase of your herds, the increase
of your cattle and the offspring of your flocks.
Blessed shall be your basket and your kneading bowl.
Blessed shall you be when you come in, and
blessed shall you be when you go out.

—Deuteronomy 28:1–6

Contents

Acknowledgments 9
Preface..11
Chapter 1:   Blessed 21
Chapter 2:   Blessed Are the Poor in Spirit for Theirs is
             the Kingdom of God..25
Chapter 3:   Blessed are those who mourn, for they shall
             be comforted. 39
Chapter 4:   Blessed Are the Meek for They Shall Inherit
             the Earth 48
Chapter 5:   Blessed Are Those Who Hunger and Thirst
             for Righteousness, for They Shall Be Filled..............58
Chapter 6:   Blessed Are the Merciful, for They Shall
             Obtain Mercy..65
Chapter 7:   Blessed Are the Pure in Heart, for They
             Shall See God...76
Chapter 8:   Blessed Are the Peacemakers, for They Shall
             be Called the Children of God 85
Chapter 9:   Blessed Are Those Who Are Persecuted for
             Righteousness Sake...92
Chapter 10: In a Nutshell 97
Resources 101

Acknowledgments

I want to thank Glenna Rowe, who when the manuscript was then at its beginning, was one of the first to proof read the raw material then gently nudged me onward. Thanks Glenna.

Transforming the manuscript from a scribbly mess into a format acceptable for the publishers viewing was my daughter-in law, Janet Jackson. Thanks Janet.

My friend Pastor Rod Ruby joined me in inspecting the text for overlooked errors. His suggestions were most appreciated. Thanks Rod.

In conclusion I want to thank my wife Anita. At the inception of writing Showers of Blessings, she was my constant encouragement to press on. Whenever, which was weekly, those enemies of pessimistic attitude or self-doubt whispered in my ear, she was the coach with the locker room motivational speech that rekindled belief within me.

To label my wife of fifty years as devoted, forgiving, faithful, committed, loving, and caring is a truth worth daily reminding myself. From the book's infancy she's been its nanny, standing watch over its progress, resolute in seeing the manuscript develop into a full-blown praise to God.

Thanks, Anita, for your seen and unseen ways of encouragement and for those long hours of reading and rereading the text before releasing the book's caregiving into the hands of the publisher.

PREFACE

Hanging Out with the Crowd

Although the world hadn't paid much attention to the fact that Easter was fast approaching, the house of God was in full anticipation. A mega church, enthusiastic over Holy Week, had written and produced an Easter musical drama. In this drama, there were scenes that depicted the life of Christ from birth to resurrection. One of the attractions of the production was a live nativity. As music from the orchestra announced the beginning, curtains at the rear of the auditorium opened, and animals, large and small, made their grand entrance. Surprised by the spectacle, the audience oohed and awed, twisted and turned, endeavoring to take it all in. With spotlights of assorted colors excitedly bouncing all over the place, the onlookers were at full attention.

First to appear were camels, slowly striding forward, jerking their heads in one direction and then another, appearing to mimic the numerous gawkers, as they sauntered through. Blanketed in silks of various colors, with decorative tassels swinging freely from their harness, fashioned the beast a bit attractive. Sheep accompanied by a caravan made up of men, women, and children were next to make their way in and through the auditorium. As the orchestra played on, the great cavalcade exited, setting the stage for Jesus and the Easter story.

Somewhere in the middle of the drama, Jesus was being tempted by the devil. The scene opened with a gloomy dimness and stirring shadows accompanied with unnerving music, giving reason to believe evil was hiding, veiled in darkness. As the drama expanded, there was but a speck of light revealing an exhausted Christ slumped over on all fours. Eerie shadows cautiously circled, giving the impression of a pack of hungry wolves moving in on their prey. Then a dull chant from within the darkness commenced, "Jesus, do a miracle, Jesus, do a miracle," and then the mantra quickened as the shadows became energized. "Jesus, do a miracle. Jesus, do a miracle. Jesus, do a miracle!"

It's with that mind-set, "Jesus, do a miracle," that the crowd on Mount Beatitude likely gathered. Certainly, some tracked Jesus from the time word spread of His healing power. Their thinking must have been similar to the woman in Matthew 9:20–21: "And suddenly, a woman who had a flow of blood for twelve years came from behind and touched the hem of His garment. For she said to herself, If only I may touch His garment, I shall be made well."

However, on that day at Mount Beatitude, Jesus was directing His healing power to a particular sickness that was a challenge to diagnose. It wasn't visible like leprosy, blindness, or a physical deformation. Jesus's focus was on the undetectable sickness known as pride, the lethal killer of the soul. Left unchecked, narcissism gorges itself until there's nothing left of a person's Christlikeness. So when Jesus addresses the crowd with, "Blessed are those who," He's offering hope to those who have the mettle to go through self-examination.

There Jesus sat, looking out among those gathered. He's in deep thought over their pain. Matthew 9:36 says, "But when He saw the multitudes, He was moved with compassion for them, because they were weary and scattered, like sheep having no shepherd." Jesus, well aware of those standing before Him, greatly needed a shepherd to guide and protect them around and through life's many entrapments. That's the very reason Christ, the Son of God, came to earth and sat with them on Mount Beatitude. The Godhead cares about the sins of His people. Hebrews 11:25 says, "He chose to be mistreated along with the people of God rather than to enjoy the fleeting pleasures of sin."

The scene that day with Jesus on Mount Beatitude was a setting of love. It was much different when God met with the people in Deuteronomy 4:11–12. It was more like a Count Dracula flick. "Then you came near and stood at the foot of the mountain, and the mountain burned with fire to the midst of heaven, with darkness, clouds, and thick darkness. And the LORD spoke to you out of the midst of the fire. You heard the sound of the words, but saw no form; you only heard a voice." From reading this passage, it can be surmised, God's mood came across as anything but loving. Piercing thunder, accompanied with colliding strikes of lightning bolts, against a backdrop of pitch darkness, had hair on necks sticking straight out. Fear replaced joy, cheerlessness replaced cheerfulness, and doubt replaced confidence. Unlike those gathered at Mount Beatitude, where love carried the moment, at Mount Horeb, fear shrouded the God experience.

This intimidating incident was designed by God to generate trepidation. It was the only means by which God of the Old Testament activated people's attention. The timeout chair didn't work. It didn't work then and doesn't appear to be working in today's age. It was spare the rod, spoil the child, and from Amos 9:2, God was in no mood to soft peddle His wishes. "Though they dig into hell, From there My hand shall take them; Though they climb up to heaven, From there I will bring them down; And though they hide themselves on top of Carmel, From there I will search and take them; Though they hide from My sight at the bottom of the sea, From there I will command the serpent, and it shall bite them." Once having the people's undivided attention at Mount Horeb, "God spoke."

You recall the movie The Wizard of Oz? The scene I'm thinking of is when the four, Dorothy, the Tin Man, the Scarecrow, and the Lion, were standing before the Great Oz. Moments before the foursome muster up enough courage to approach his throne, the Great Oz thunders out, "Who are you?"

Dorothy, terrified and traumatized, speaks. "I…If you please. I…I am Dorothy." As she continues, she nervously gestures by looking back at her companions.

"The small and meek. We've come to ask you."

Before Dorothy could utter another word, rumblings, accompanied with flashes of lightning, filled the chamber. It was the unmistakable announcement the Great Oz was on his throne. Immediately following the Oz's magnificent introduction, he roars, "Silence."

That's the spectacle I picture of those assembled at Mount Horeb. They were terrorized by God's manifestation. That's not the picture of God we get in Jesus at Mount Beatitude. So before continuing, we must have a clear understanding of the character of God, both in God the Son and God the Father. If not, our thinking will have God of the Old Testament portrayed as Jekyll, and Jesus of the New testament portrayed as Hyde.

Turning to chapters 11 through 13 of Exodus, God has called on Pharaoh to let the people of Israel go. Upon the ruler's refusal, Israel's God rained down plague upon plague on the King and his kingdom. Nonetheless, the monarch deeply entrenched in pride, challenges Israel's God one last time, and lives to regret it, as the Judge of all passes through Egypt. Not pass through as we think of, just passing through. God's passing through would affect every living thing. Every first born, animal or human, stood the chance of dying before sunup. If not aware of what's taking place, we'll miss God of the Old Testament's desire for intimacy with His people.

Exodus 12:3–7 says, "On the tenth of this month every man shall take for himself a lamb, according to the house of his father, a lamb for a household. And if the household is too small for the lamb, let him and his neighbor next to his house take it according to the number of the persons; according to each man's need you shall make your count for the lamb. Your lamb shall be without blemish, a male of the first year. You may take it from the sheep or from the goats. Now you shall keep it until the fourteenth day of the same month. Then the whole assembly of the congregation of Israel shall kill it at twilight. Then they shall take some of the blood and put it on the two doorposts and the lintel of the houses in which they eat it."

The plan was uncomplicated. God promised to "pass over" those houses marked in blood. The blood would be their protection and shelter from destruction. It is here we must see God of the Old Testament, as God the loving rescuer. God of the Old Testament is the God in Jesus that warmly sat with the crowd on the Mount

Beatitude. Jesus said in John 14:9b, "He who has seen Me has seen the Father."

Hanging on the cross at Calvary was God. The Judge and the Savior are the same. It was God who moved through Egypt, to pronounce judgment, and it was God who passed over Israelite homes rescuing the obedient. And finally, it's God in Christ that came to rescue believers by way of the cross. It's a joint indwelling, God in the Father and God in the Son. It must be understood the two cannot be separated. John 17:21–23 says, "that they all may be one, as You, Father, are in Me, and I in You; that they also may be one in Us, that the world may believe that You sent Me. And the glory which You gave Me I have given them, that they may be one just as We are one: I in them, and You in Me."

When Christ lovingly sat with the crowd on Mount Beatitude, He's not an independent third party of the Trinity. It's not Jesus the good guy, inspiring the crowd, while the bad guy, God of the Old Testament, is somewhere calling down hell on some pitiable soul. God in Jesus, murky as that statement may be, warmly sits with the crowd, majesty and mystery in three persons, as God relates in love and language.

And so, it was God in Jesus, sitting with the crowd at Mount Beatitude, giving guidance to spiritually lost people. The crowd was all too familiar with their botched struggles against fleshly indulgence. They had firsthand experience on what disowning God looked like. The Apostle Peter's denial of knowing Jesus had nothing on them. They needed to be unshackled from guilt, eclipsing any chance of hope. And there sat God in Jesus, the one they sinned against, doing the rescuing.

Before joining the crowd to hear Jesus's message, I reflect on an experience that will assist in understanding the point Jesus will be stressing. That point is this: Jesus is the only way for salvation. Christ is our only hope for forgiveness of sins we've committed against God. Jesus is the single means by which we can be rescued from hell. With that said, I share with you the following.

In the spring of 2015, parts of the Midwest received a taste of what Southeast Asia experiences during monsoon season. Storm clouds repeatedly rolled in, collapsed, roll in, and collapsed. The continuous downpour sent families living in the lowlands scurrying for higher ground. Corn fields were converted into jet boat's playgrounds, while ponds of many shapes and sizes developed overnight. At last, the torrential rain waned, leaving in its wake stories of great magnitude. For me, it was the observance of what I term, "the achievement of the cross."

Our pet dog, Three Colors, was approaching her second birthday party. Her youth and oomph compelled me daily to walk her, rain or shine. Our home in Ohio sets on the banks of Indian Lake State Park. Running alongside one section of the park is a bike path. The path snakes its way nearer the water's edge at some points and twists away at others. Due to heavy rain, the lake swelled, overflowing its banks. It stretches the length of a football field, where the land is higher in elevation, and there the pathway was dry. Where the land is bowl shaped, the walkway disappeared under five to six inches of water, creating a danger for vertebrates with gills. Spawning fish could be fooled into thinking the overflow that formed small ponds were the shallows of the lake. However, once the lake returned within its banks, the asphalt pathway became a blockade separating fish from the lake.

That's exactly what happened. Colors and I came upon a large fish duped into thinking it was in the shallows of the shoreline but, in fact, was trapped in a small pocket of water, with no way of escape. Exhausted from struggling to swim in ankle-deep water, the fish rested across a steel grated manhole cover. Water trekking down a hillside ravine running across its gills was the only means that kept the fish alive.

For the longest time, Colors and I stood motionless, staring down at the drama of death unfolding. Witnessing demise is heart-wrenching, be it animal or mortal. In fact, this past week, my neighbor's family pet of ten years died. Numerous years in the past, following the evening meal, my neighbor and his dog journeyed to the woodland behind their residence. The last few months, complication brought on by the dog's age all but ended their cherished ritual. To prolong the inevitable my neighbor built a cart to pull behind his yard tractor. His pet would start out walking somewhat frisky, but by mid journeys end he required the cart to complete their walk. This past Sunday morning, my neighbor found his pet dead. To demonstrate his admiration for his faithful companion, my neighbor wrapped the dog's body in a blanket, laying him in the cart. Then, as in days gone by, the two of them travelled one last trip around their sacred ground. Witnessing the ending of life, be it mammal or mankind, will most certainly stir emotions.

So there I stood by the fish, motionless, mesmerized from the drama of death unfolding. Finally, I reasoned I must allow nature, extremely cruel at times, to have its way. It was in fact, merely a fish. Leaving anything dying isn't in my DNA; nonetheless, calling Colors to my side, we reluctantly headed home.

The following morning, Colors and I again choose the path less traveled by those taking their daily walks. Puddles of water on the walking path encouraged walkers with common sense to consider an alternate course. Not all had common sense, as Colors and I again decided on the path from the previous day. As we walked I mulled over the question, would the hefty fish be there or had the creatures of the night feasted on the helpless. The whole thing seemed lacking good sense, pondering if some fish would be dead or alive. Who cares! In fact, in my automobile that morning, on the way to the walkway, I veered to avoid a dead cat. The only thought that entered my mind then was don't run over the corpse. Messy, messy, messy.

Once into the walk, we approached the area of the manhole. No fish. Instantaneously, I launch into an earnest search. Here I am, supposedly a mature grown male, frolicking in the muck, and for what, a big fish? I first thought of it as silly. Then the word stupid crossed my mind. Yes, that's it, stupid, exceedingly stupid. During the chastising conversation with myself, I was awakened to the possibility of someone observing my display of foolishness. Nonchalantly, I went from thrashing up and down the weedy edge, like some mad man, to a leisurely stroll, hoping I would appear captivated over nature's scenery. Then, out of the corner of one eye, I scanned the landscape for any peeping Tom's. Once confident the coast was clear, I wasted no time hurling myself back into the weightier thing of life, searching for the big fish of yesterday.

Yesterday's strong flow of water that moved through the grassy ravine was now but a trickle. And there, half submersed in a thick weedy area, with barely enough water to cover its gills, rested my exhausted friend, I mean fish. Little did the fish know, it was dead. It may have appeared to be living as it's gills were moving, but in reality it was as good as dead. Separating the fish and the place from where it grew up was that dreaded exposed asphalt pathway. That exact asphalt pathway she swam over days earlier. The water moved back into its banks, and the hope of swimming in the deep again, the hope of another stimulating spawning experience, would be no more. She was as good as dead. Nothing in the fish's power could have brought hope to her bleakness.

I don't recall the number of times I repeated, "Leave nature alone." I do, however, recall my rebuttal. "I am pro-life, period." I would be the fish's solitary source of hope, redeemer if you will, rescuer for sure. There, lying on the rocks by the shore, was a muddy cloth book bag. The carrier was perfect for the rescue. With Colors impatiently jumping at my side, fancying investigating our finding, I slide the bag over the carp's head similar to putting on socks. Then once crossing the asphalt pathway, to the water's edge, I turned the book bag upside down, a splash, and the mission was accomplished.

Once successfully aiding and abetting the fish its freedom and discarded the muddy bag, we resumed our walk. Reaching our walks designated halfway point, we turned and headed back. Passing the area where the adventure came to its end, Colors stopped walking. Spotting the muddy book bag lying on the shoreline, she wanted to have one last look. We did, and once satisfied the rescue was accomplished, we turned to leave. This time, I picked up the mud caked bag, as there was a story to share with my wife.

Once home, I went straight to the furnace room where the utility sink is stationed. First priority was to wash the foul-smelling mud-caked bag. During the washing I discovered, in large print, the word LOVE stitched in sequins on one side. Bam, it hit me. The fish incident was a huge comparison of God in Christ, redeeming, or rescuing sin-troubled people. Earlier I thought, if hope didn't come soon for the fish, the dead man's float would have become reality. That statement is also true for mankind.

Both man and that fish have gone astray. Man has lost his way. It's the very reason God in the Son sat with the crowd that day on the mount. Like the gilled vertebrate, man's only hope is to receive a power outside themselves. 1 Peter 1:3 says, "Blessed be the God and Father of our Lord Jesus Christ, who according to His abundant mercy has begotten us again to a living hope through the resurrection of Jesus Christ from the dead."

"Living hope" isn't something that pertains to the future. Living hope is confidence for today, now. The Bible's idea of hope is very different from our normal perception of promise. The fish in desperation may have been thinking, I hope a tsunami makes its way here, real soon. It's a desire for something the fish is uncertain of attaining. On the other hand, Peter calls Jesus, "living hope." Living hope has power to produce real change in lives. If the crowd listening to Jesus that day on the mount doesn't receive outside help, just as the fish did, they're doomed. Living hope begins when we cease pinning our dream for happiness on wishful thinking. Instead, we're encouraged to pursue Christ Jesus as our sole confidence for salvation.

If we choose Christ over all sorts of instant gratifications, Jesus promises blessedness. We say, bring it on! Yet with a promise of that magnitude, we must ask this question. Why isn't there pandemonium scurrying to Jesus to attain this promised gladness? For sure, happiness is undoubtedly the quest of all mankind. And to add to that, John 16:22 says, "Your heart will rejoice, and your joy no one will take from you." If happiness is the goal of mankind, why isn't there a Black Friday scramble to attain Jesus's way to happiness? The answer is this. The sermon on the mount promises happiness only to those who live life based on Christ' teachings. There lies the rub. Many believers are not convinced that Jesus is the only way to fulfillment. Taking a survey of my neighborhood, it would be effortless to surmise that happiness, for the mainstream, comes by way of stuff. In or around homes are numerous cars, boats, motorbikes, four-wheelers, snowmobiles, trucks, and an assortment of other things inside the residence. And every Christmas, there's a human stampede in shopping centers, chasing the elusive. Although the frantic search for happiness has left many lying on the sofa of some therapist, the quest for instant fulfillment trudges on.

It was no different for those in the crowd at Mount Beatitude. An elevated hopefulness moved through the crowd as Jesus began to speak. Running through the minds of those in attendance must have been, would they be part of Jesus miracle making? They most certainly could have been, if they had grasped the type of phenomenon Jesus was ready to perform. Nevertheless, it wasn't a marvel such as changing water into wine, healing lepers, or empowering the lame to walk. For sure, Jesus was engrossed in miracle making, but it was by way of renewing of their minds. For when the mind realizes Jesus and Jesus alone is the means for everlasting fulfillment, the quest for the spectacular loses its attraction. Jesus repeatedly said, "Blessed shall you be." And the blessing was then, and is today, when we have peace with God in Jesus. Now, let's join the crowd as Jesus unfolds the meaning of blessed shall you be!

Chapter 1

Blessed

A friend of mine, after persevering through an extremely difficult year economically and on the marriage front, said, "How blessed am I!" Before progressing into Jesus's message on the mountain, I take a moment to examine Jesus "blessed" statements He repeatedly uttered while addressing the disciples and the crowd. The passage in Matthew 5:1–12 reads as follows:

> And seeing the multitudes, He went up on a mountain, and when He was seated His disciples came to Him. Then He opened His mouth and taught them, saying: Blessed are the poor in spirit, for theirs is the kingdom of heaven. Blessed are those who mourn, for they shall be comforted. Blessed are the meek, for they shall inherit the earth. Blessed are those who hunger and thirst for righteousness, for they shall be filled. Blessed are the merciful, for they shall obtain mercy. Blessed are the pure in heart, for they shall see God. Blessed are the peacemakers, for they shall be called sons of God. Blessed are those who are persecuted for righteousness' sake, for theirs is the kingdom of heaven. Blessed are you when they revile and persecute you, and say all kinds of

evil against you falsely for My sake. Rejoice and be exceedingly glad, for great is your reward in heaven, for so they persecuted the prophets who were before you.

The word "blessed" in the above passage clearly means happy. Not happy as in laughter, giggles, or a smiley face. That type of happiness comes about when life is sweet to the taste: it's a spontaneous response to a temporary pleasure that's up for grabs. Maybe the chances one takes in life will bring happiness. Then again, maybe they won't. It's a flip of the coin. The chance for happiness may start off exciting and then turn into an oppressive yoke.

The prodigal son, for example, stormed out into the highways and byways, determined to realize, once and for all, "happiness." Luke 15:11–14 says, "Then He said: 'A certain man had two sons. And the younger of them said to his father, father, give me the portion of goods that falls to me.' So, he divided to them his livelihood. And not many days after, the younger son gathered all together, journeyed to a far country, and there wasted his possessions with prodigal (reckless) living. But when he had spent all, there arose a severe famine in that land and he began to be in want."

It's great reading because we find ourselves in the story. The disappointing ending to the son's pursuit for lasting fulfillment doesn't surprise us. In one way or another, we've been there. As you may recall, the prodigal lad, or the wasteful son, went through all the wampum at his fingertips. His seeking happiness, something for which we all strive, was his top priority. With a pocket full of money, a mind filled with assorted possibilities and youth on his side, it was full speed ahead. Nevertheless, when he arrived at the end of his rainbow, not even the bowl that supposedly would hold his dreams was anywhere to be found. Surprise, surprise!

The prodigal's story is our story, at least the part of recklessly searching for happiness. From the time of Adam, men and women alike have preferred the broader way of unearthing that elusive ecstasy. In addition, it wasn't due to the prodigal's youthfulness that had him searching in all the wrong places. King Solomon, long after his boyish charm disappeared, was enthusiastically investigating different paths to happiness. He made the prodigal son's attempt at achieving fulfillment appear as a beginner's performance. Nor did Solomon's formula for acquiring happiness need copyright protection. It began with self-indulgence and ended with more of the same. And by no means can Solomon be charged with being a slacker when it came to pursuing happiness.

To begin with, his accumulative wealth was massive. If money and power were the only means by which to measure a person's worth, Solomon was at the top of his class. And there's no need to investigate Solomon's statement in Ecclesiastes 2:10 that says, "And whatever my eyes desired I did not keep from them. I kept my heart from no pleasure." The reason there's no need to investigate is found in 1 Kings 11:3: "And he had seven hundred wives, princesses, and three hundred concubines; and his wives turned away his heart." I suspect Solomon's mother over the years had chitchats with her son regarding the birds and bees. Her chats, I also suspect, fell on deaf ears. Solomon's sights were set on attaining that elusive experience of being genuinely 100 percent blissful. And women, lots of women, were part of his plan.

However, as time went on, Solomon waved the white flag of surrender. Weary from his gallant endeavor to realize happiness, he faintly utters in Ecclesiastes 12:8, "Vanity of vanities, all is vanity." The word vanity means emptiness. To decode Solomon's statement of "vanity of vanities," I venture to say means, if you're searching for fulfillment using the world's formula for success, you labor in vain.

In the Beatitudes message, Jesus teaches true happiness is a matter of the heart. Christ's words are echoed in 1 Samuel 16:7: "Man looks at the outward appearance, but the Lord looks at the heart." We read from time to time where a person marries someone who seems frail and unattractive. Not for material gain, but through encountering their inner beauty. So when man has a heart toward God over all other worldly sways, he's discovered the truth where genuine happiness is to be found.

Jesus's message points to an internal change as the means by which fulfillment comes about. Proverbs 4:23 says, "Watch over your heart…for from it flows the springs of life." "Heart" refers not to the organ pounding behind one's chest. Rather, it's the entire personality and character. 2 Corinthians 10:5 says, "bringing every thought into captivity to the obedience of Christ." Solomon nearing the finish line of life on earth foolishly continued seeking happiness through externals. The question before us is, are we that much different? A truthful self-examination will often reveal we're not convinced God is the only supplier of a fulfilled life. As for Solomon, he left no earthly stone unturned in pursuit for bliss. And if not vigilant, we, like Solomon, will chase true happiness in all the wrong places.

Watching over one's heart is a huge undertaking. Deuteronomy 4:9 says, "Only take heed to yourself, and diligently keep yourself, lest you forget the things your eyes have seen, and lest they depart from your heart all the days of your life." Keeping guard over the soul is a full-time responsibility. Reliance on God rather than self is a daily battle. Yet if we're to realize contentment, a renewing of the mind must take place. The psalmist writes in the first part of Psalm 31:15, "My times are in your hand." All the varied happenings that take place throughout life, be they delightful or woeful, are under the watchful eye of the one possessing supreme authority. When we genuinely embrace God being intricately involved in all our life experiences, inward joy will be the byproduct.

God, not life experiences, produces lasting happiness. God, not worldly possessions or achievements, satisfies the quest for contentment. With that, let's listen in on Jesus's first "Blessed are you" statement.

Chapter 2

Blessed Are the Poor in Spirit for Theirs
is the Kingdom of God

Matthew 5:1

I haven't run into many people who yearn to be impoverished financially. Which prompted me to ask the question, how is it that Jesus proclaims the poor, pitiable, and destitute in spirit are blessed? My answer comes by way of a friend who painfully came to understand that soul poverty is truly a blessing. His story goes as follows.

My friend was fighting for his life. His adversary, the narcotic heroin, was unwavering in bringing his life to an end.

His journey into addiction began simple enough. He and two friends, one a female, were sitting in the two boys' apartment. The female was an aunt to my friend's roommate. All three were no strangers to the mood-altering drug, marijuana. Their conversation that Saturday morning was no different than at any other time, music, artists, and street news. Without breaking the flow of their chat, the aunt offered the boys a "ride on the train." On the street, the name heroin is seldom verbalized. When voiced in public, heroin goes by safer names: antifreeze, Big H, brown sugar, golden girls, H, horse, junk, poison, smack, sweet dreams, tar, and the train. The request was no different from being offered a piece of candy. At the time, my friend had no concept he was literally boarding the ride of his life or, better still, the ride very possibly to end his life.

An agreement was struck before taking the train ride. Aunt, the provider, wouldn't live in their apartment. The thinking behind this idea was if Aunt didn't live with them, there wouldn't be a close connection to boarding the next heroin "train". Once in agreement, Aunt, with the steadiness of a surgeon's hand, gently placed a razor blade between the thumb and index finger. With precision, she divided the brown powder into three equal lines atop the face of a compact mirror. I emphasize the word equal, as all eyes were engrossed on the drug being equally distributed. The aunt's steady hand gave evidence she'd boarded the "train" earlier that day. Otherwise, failure to feed her addiction would've left her with the appearance of a butcher franticly hacking at the brown crystal, desperate on getting the magic into her system.

Leaning his head parallel to the floor, my friend placed one end of a rolled-up dollar bill into his nostril. Inhaling through his nose, he slowly guided the tube down the thin line of powder. He didn't' recall the moment sober consciousness vanished, but he knew to the minute the moment his personality flip-flopped from being a person of willpower to lacking in self discipline. From then on, boarding the next drug train was solely chasing that initial trip of elation. Hounding after euphoria, a new priority emerged. Primary importance such as rent money remained the same. One might reason he was thinking rather clearly, until discovering food went from a tie for first to third place. It was money for the rent and money for the exhilarated ride came one and two, and not necessarily in that order.

I'll skip all that transpired in my friend's life during the succeeding two years by stating there was a second-deep need demanding his attention, peace of mind. He yearned for those continuous out of control runaway thoughts to subside. He erroneously reasoned he found the means by which to do so. The lie put across to Adam and Eve was the lie restated to him. Genesis 3:4–7 says, "Then the serpent said to the woman, 'You will not surely die. For God knows that in the day you eat of it your eyes will be opened and you will be like God, knowing good and evil.' So, when the woman saw that the tree was good for food, that it was pleasant to the eyes, and a tree desirable to make one wise, she took of its fruit and ate. She also gave to her husband with her, and he ate. Then the eyes of both of them were opened, and they knew that they were naked. And they sewed fig leaves together and made themselves coverings." The disgraced first couple immediately went into hiding as did my friend. He hid from himself the truth with a veil of lies, carelessly reasoning he could exit the drug train at his choosing. As time passed, the veil became threadbare, and the shameful truth was for all to see, including himself.

Wretched

At twenty-one, he understood himself to be appalling to God, family, and self. I pause in the story to consider you and me. Recognizing we are wretched, having no righteousness of our own to offer God, becomes huge in experiencing God's blessings. My friend cried out to God as the tax collector did in Luke 18:13, "O God, be thou merciful to me, a sinner," or when the Apostle Paul humbled himself in Romans 7:24, "O wretched man that I am! Who will deliver me from this body of death?" When you and I lament to God over times we've been the prodigal son, blessed are we. To be conscious of our need for His mercy is evidence the living God is active in our lives. It's not with despair the faithful cry out to God. Despair signals loss of hope. Christ purged hopelessness from us, and in its place He unveiled grace upon grace, divine favor upon divine favor.

I recall times I foolishly sought God's favor through proudly living life through asceticism, absent any remorse for my sins that nailed Christ to the cross. Isaiah 66:2 brings to light such irrational thinking. No need to run out and accomplish some feat of good works bringing about instant gratification. Isaiah 57:15 gives the blueprint for resuscitating a soul on life support. "For thus says the High and Lofty One Who inhabits eternity, whose name is Holy: I dwell in the high and holy place, with him who has a contrite and humble spirit, to revive the spirit of the humble, and to revive the heart of the contrite ones." God is pure, wholesome, and holy; nevertheless, He vindicates the sinner who acknowledges having nothing to bring before His throne other than brokenness. Now, back to my friend's fessing up to being among the addicted, having nothing to bring before God as a means of peacemaking.

Please, somebody stop this train

My friend was marooned on an island of hopelessness with no help in sight. Playing his guitar, he would sing the lyrics of the song, "Badfish," sung by Sublime.

> Ain't got no money to spend
> I hope the night will never end
> Lord knows I'm weak
> Won't somebody get me off of this reef

Singing those lyrics was his cry for help. But the glitch was those he cried out to were themselves on the reef.

Now or never, jump!

Deciding to withdraw cold turkey was my friend's means of terminating his suicide ride. He asks a street acquaintance to drive him to a wooded area far removed from any so-called friends or neon lights, as both held influence on his judgment.

Once in the country, the driver pulled alongside a stretch of woods. Putting the car into neutral, the driver offered one last pull on a joint as a gesture of sympathy. A slight almost undetected negative head nod told of the weightiness of the moment. As he closed the car door behind him, both knew their association was forever terminated, never to be sought after again.

As car and driver pulled away, my friend eyed the vehicle down the road until it was but a speck. Now alone, with a small tent, four sandwiches, and a gallon of water, he despondently turned and trudged wearily into the woodland. I cannot help but think of the astronaut's words when stepping on the surface of the moon, with a few variations. It was one small step for the nonaddicted one gigantic leap for some lonesome kid fighting for his life. It's not that he hadn't contemplated chucking the whole idea as craziness, for he had. For weeks on end, he clashed with mental tormentors. His weapon in fighting the repressions off was reflecting on his mother. Mom was the thread he hung onto for his reason to live.

Wandering deeper into the woods, his chest tightened as beads of moister appeared on his forehead signaling the conflict had now commenced. Out of nowhere, fear blindsided him. He wasn't in dread of being alone in a dark woodland bursting with eerie night sounds. The apprehension came from the mental and physical hostility soon to be upon him. He was squaring off with an opponent that had beat him to a pulp numerous times in the past. However, on this night, it was winner take all, a fight to the finish. Suicide awaited, but not before facing this evil titan one final time. Unbeknownst to him, the God who brought David's mighty Goliath to his knees was his fight manager.

His physical body's annoyance at being denied the magical powder turned to wrath. By nightfall, evil screams from within him became excruciating. Mental attacks strikingly similar to what Jesus went through in Matthew 4:1. "Jesus was led by the Spirit into the wilderness to be tempted by the devil." It wasn't the agonizing forty days that Jesus stood toe to toe with Satan, nonetheless, three days, dawn to dusk, and throughout the night, withdrawal symptoms viciously assaulted him as Satan battered his prey. God's words in 1 Corinthians 13:10 says, "No temptation has overtaken you except such as is common to man; but God is faithful, who will not allow you to be tempted beyond what you are able, but with the temptation will also make the way of escape, that you may be able to bear it."

God's way of escape for my friend was through frequent and vicious retching. Vomiting took his mind off of everything, and once the body discharged all solids, dry heaving followed. At this point, the words from Romans 8:28 must be heard. "And we know that all things work together for good to those who love God."

Following days of nonstop anguish, calm commenced to envelope him. His traumatized shivering lessoned, incessant gagging subsided, and his tortured psyche lay exhausted. Mind you, there would be no joy in the morning celebration. Nonetheless, following days of being mentally and physically mugged, he remained, if not standing, victorious. The fight was suspended, not over by any means; nevertheless, he prevailed to experience that amazing thing called hope.

Slowly exiting the wooded battleground, he willed his body down country roads, musing over what to do next. He was victorious, but no ticker tape parade was awaiting him nor one trusted friend in which to confide. Nothing! I take that back, there was something awaiting him, a warrant for his arrest. Needing money for the drug train, he endeavored selling the magical powder. Entering the police station, he announced who he was by uttering, "You have a warrant for my arrest." It was another one of those small step experiences, one small step for the innocent, and one huge step for the guilty.

Following a few days in jail and a court date, he was released. With no place to go, he roamed the streets until coming upon an uninhabited fair ground. Sitting alone on a bench, staring out at a world appearing cold and unconcerned, he contemplated living and dying. Then an abrupt sound from his rear caused him to quickly turn. When he did, there, on the wooden back support of the bench he was sitting on, was a memorial plate. Reading the engraving, his eyes teared up. He knew the name to be a neighborhood friend of his past, whose death came by way of suicide. Immediately, he stood and abruptly headed out in the opposite direction, again running from the past.

Unconsciously, he headed for his mom's house. Nearing her home, nausea again enveloped him. His queasiness was from the thought of confessing he lied regarding money missing from her home, and secondly, he was a drug addict. How true are those words, it's darkest just before the dawn.

Years have passed since my friend last boarded the heroin ride. To his credit, he's grasped the truth each of us must eventually succumb to: we've made one huge mess of our lives. Self-examination is where the confessional ball is launched from. Character searching is healing, provided we've the courage to examine ourselves up against God's holy word. Poor in spirit means knowing our wretched self, confessing our need for a redeemer, and then sincerely praying to be transformed.

When Jesus addressed the twelve apostles and the crowd on the mount with, "Blessed are the poor in spirit, for theirs is the kingdom of heaven," Jesus was saying this is the road leading to happiness. For happiness to become reality, we must not only act differently but think differently. 2 Corinthians 10:5b says, "Bringing every thought into captivity to the obedience of Christ."

Acknowledging spiritual bankruptcy is the first assault on pride, the roadblock, to sanctification. Philippians 3:10 says, "that I may know Him and the power of His resurrection, and the fellowship of His sufferings." The very idea of knowing the Creator is wild. Yet it's the experience every person encounter's who's been brought out of the darkness of arrogance into God's marvelous light. Know for sure, recognizing debauchery in your personality is evidence you're in the hands of God the potter.

Until we recognize, accept, and admit our brokenness, we'll journey through life deficient of intimacy with the living God. And be certain, the poverty Jesus speaks of isn't poor materialistically. It's poverty of the soul, which declares, I cannot, I cannot on my own achievements make peace with God. Isaiah 66:2 says, "'For all those things My hand has made, and all those things exist,' Says the LORD. 'But on this one will I look: On him who is poor and of a contrite spirit, and who trembles at My word'."

It's the spiritually broken, the poor in spirit, whom God announces "blessed are you."

A striking illustration of the contrast between contrite and proud is found in Luke's gospel chapter 18:10–14: "Two men went up to the temple to pray, one a Pharisee and the other a tax collector. The Pharisee stood and prayed thus with himself, 'God, I thank You that I am not like other men—extortioners, unjust, adulterers, or even as this tax collector. I fast twice a week; I give tithes of all that I possess.' And the tax collector, standing afar off, would not so much as raise his eyes to heaven, but beat his breast, saying, 'God, be merciful to me a sinner!' I tell you, this man went down to his house justified rather than the other; for everyone who exalts himself will be humbled, and he who humbles himself will be exalted."

Both men entered the temple to pray. However, the Pharisee's self-righteous declarations gave evidence his praying was either out of duty, habit, or hobby, with similarities of rehearsing a speech. His praying starts off in a sincere manner, "God, I thank you." However, that's the last time God's name is mentioned, one and done. From there on, his agenda is about self. There's a song entitled, "I Wanna Talk about Me." And the lyrics fit the Pharisee spot on.

> I wanna talk about me
> Wanna talk about I
> Wanna talk about number one
> What I think, what I like, what I know, what I want, what I see
> I like talking about you, usually, but occasionally
> I wanna talk about me.

What didn't cross the Pharisee's mind standing in the presence of the glorious God was, "woe is me." His reaction was far removed from Isaiah's in the book of Isaiah 6:1–5:

> "In the year that King Uzziah died, I saw the Lord sitting on a throne, high and lifted up, and the train of His robe filled the temple. Above it stood seraphim; each one had six wings: with two he covered his face, with two he covered his feet, and with two he flew. And one cried to another and said:
> Holy, holy, holy is the Lord of hosts; the whole earth is full of His glory! And the posts of the door were shaken by the voice of him who cried out, and the house was filled with smoke." So, I said: "Woe is me, for I am undone! Because I am a man of unclean lips, and I dwell in the midst of a people of unclean lips."

Isaiah came face-to-face with the truth regarding his soiled soul by simply uttering, "woe is me." Keep in mind, it was the Lord who commissioned Isaiah as a messenger to confront God's spiritually insensitive people. Isaiah was, so to speak, in God's inner circle. And to hear him utter, "woe is me, for I am undone," illustrates how essential Christ is when approaching God.

The Pharisee, on the other hand, was light years from seeing himself necessitating the mercy of God. His thinking was much like Jack in the children's poem, "Little Jack Horner."

> Little Jack Horner
> Sat in the corner,
> Eating a Christmas pie;
> He put in his thumb,
> And pulled out a plum,
> And said, "What a good boy am I!"

That's the attitude the Pharisee had in his spiritual life. His conception of himself was far removed from what Peter saw in himself in Luke 5:8. "He fell down at Jesus' knees, saying, 'Depart from me, for I am a sinful man, O Lord!'" Mercy was the last thing on the mind of this member of the Jewish sect as he was engrossed in nobler thoughts, such as commending himself for his virtue.

Nonetheless, Jesus's message at the mountain was inspirational and uplifting to those who owned up to spiritual struggling. Genuine regret over one's depravity is the dawn of knowing God, and knowing God is the epitome of life on earth. In place of strapping shame to their backs, Jesus declared, "blessed are you". Read these inspiring words in Psalm 34:18: "The LORD is 'near' to those who have a broken heart, and saves such as have a contrite spirit."

While in prison ministry, I met Lorenzo, who was released some ten years after residing for eons behind reformatory's steel bars. We've remained in contact through letters, phone calls, and occasional outings. The following is his story of being blessed by his poor in spirit attitude.

As Lorenzo's time of incarceration neared completion, his excitement intensified. The penal institution offered classes to inmates to assist in their rehabilitation before being released. As an incentive for enrolling, one day would be deducted from his sentence for each class taken. That was incentive enough to spur my friend to enroll in whatever topics were offered.

Electrified over his upcoming discharge, he gave away personal belongings, keeping nothing to remind him of those lost years of his life. Then it happened. Two days before being released, an inmate mail carrier delivered a parcel having the effect of a pipe bomb explosion. Boldly printed on the top right-hand corner was, "Office of the Warden". As the mail carrier moved further down C-block, Lorenzo returned to his bunk, opening the letter suspiciously. Anything coming from the keeper of the prison was to be dealt with skeptically. "Upon preparing your papers for your discharge, a calculation error has been realized. Your new release date is set back to September 10, 2008." A fifteen-day correction was added to his supposed release time. He read, reread, and read again while mentally free falling. His emotions shattered like a water glass crashing upon a cement floor. Mirroring a caged lion, Lorenzo began pacing and mumbling hate.

At the time, Lorenzo was light years from what the Apostle Peter wrote in 1 Peter 2:2: "When He was reviled, He did not revile in return; when He suffered, He did not threaten, but committed Himself to Him who judges righteously." Lorenzo invited Christ into his heart, and what is more, he was living proof of the promise in Philippians 1:6. "He who has begun a good work in you will complete it until the day of Jesus Christ." However, sanctification is a process, and on this day, he needed all the time God allotted in his being transformed.

When the call came for lights out, Lorenzo lowered his wearied body to the edge of the bunk and quietly sobbed. I say quietly, as the inmate in the next cell must never hear him cry. As tears collected at the point of his nose, then dropped to the floor, splattering much like his emotions, he whispered, "I can't do it, Lord. I can't do it. Hate swells within me, I desire to turn the cheek but inside me screams, hate 'em, hate 'em. Holy God, please help me. I cannot…love those who did this to me."

There, in his last murmur of "I cannot" is to be poor in spirit. He knew the truth regarding who he wasn't. He also knew his greatest need, God's mercy through Jesus Christ. That, my friend, is to be poor in spirit.

During those fifteen additional days of torment, Lorenzo leaned heavily on prayer. First, his plea was for God to stop the stampede of his runaway mind. When that flopped, he entreated for a heart of forgiveness. Again, nothing. In retrospect, he would say, those days of torment revealed a new appreciation of Jesus Christ dying for his sins. He well understood it wasn't he and Christ who brought about salvation but Christ alone.

In 1940, Jonny Mercer wrote the lyrics to "Fools Rush in Where Angels Fear to Tread." How many fools there are in the church who've subscribed to salvation through achievement. If not on guard to such foolishness, we'll mimic the Pharisee, himself a fool, believing, "my, my, my, what a good boy am I." Such rationale is erroneously taught by the majority of religions. For example, St. Augustine, so proud of his intellect, said brainpower held him back from believing. Or Martin Luther, who spent his youthful days alone in a monastery, committed to asceticism as his means to enlightenment. Both were humbled when uncovering that Jesus Christ stood alone as the single means for salvation.

To be poor in spirit is to turn from self-reliance, confessing dependence on Christ, and Christ alone. To be poor in spirit is more than an occurrence now and then. Isaiah 57:15 says, "For thus says the high and lofty One who inhabits eternity, whose name is Holy: "I dwell in the high and holy place, with him who has a contrite and humble spirit." The words "with him who has" refer to the person who lives daily, hour by hour, in the need of God's grace and upon His dependency.

Lorenzo, upon being notified of this somber news, shot me a letter. His words were similar to Paul's in 2 Corinthians 4:8 paraphrased. "I am hard-pressed, Max, yet not defeated; I feel like I've been swindled, but I remain positive; mistreated and there's nothing I can do about it, but I am not forsaken; struck down, and I mean hard, but not destroyed." Humility prevents the folly of self-righteousness.

Upon being released, Lorenzo desperately required God's lifting Spirit in those challenging days. Freedom brought obligations, and with a felony strapped to his back, black in color, and scarcely out from behind bars, the odds of finding work were a thousand to one against him. Faced with two solid weeks of repeatedly being denied employment, he signed up with a temporary employment agency. At last, a spark of hope flickered as he was to report to a pizza factory. Unbeknownst to Lorenzo, temporary services sent twelve others to the same location for the few openings. To be chosen depended on where he stood in line when the doors opened. The early bird got the worm. Lorenzo's difficulty was city transit, as it was his only means of travel, and from where he lived, getting to the factory meant changing buses numerous times. It goes without saying, he seldom got the worm. When selected, the factories quitting time went beyond city buses' last run of the night, leaving him no choice but to spend the night in the factory's cafeteria.

Irrespective, the struggle to acquire employment and the consequences of no paycheck kept him pushing. He phoned early one winter morning returning home from again being on the short end of the stick. Those inner voices that affirmed his total worthlessness when incarcerated were viciously assaulting him as he defeatedly returned home. Paul's words in Philippians 1:14 were Lorenzo's daily mandatory nutrition. "I press toward the goal for the prize of the upward call of God in Christ Jesus."

Answering my phone one morning, I immediately heard singing. "The driver of the bus says move on back, move on back, move on back, the driver of the bus says move on back, all through the town." Then I heard Lorenzo laughing, truly laughing. Absent was any anger pointing to God's seemingly indifference to his struggles. He would say God owed him nothing. He was joyful to be waiting for a bus as a free man. He practiced 2 Corinthians 6:10: "As sorrowful, yet always rejoicing; as poor, yet making many rich; as having nothing, and yet possessing all things."

At long last, Lorenzo found steady employment at an industrial plant, although the first year he was under the title, "part-time." Owing to his strong work ethic and dependability, he was eligible for full time. That meant a magnificent pay increase with essential benefits. Elated, Lorenzo phoned, going on and on about being invited to join the company.

SHOWERS OF BLESSINGS

There wasn't much to the interview. Minimal paper work, some oral questions, and out the door he went. He'd be notified in a few days. First thing Monday morning, a loud speaker summoned Lorenzo to report to personnel. Hearing his name announced prompted a rush of nervousness. His nerves kicked in akin to grade school days when his name shot out over the intercom to report to the principal's office. Endeavoring to move beyond unenthusiastic thinking, he quickly dropped his paint brush and headed for the personnel office.

The confidence he enjoyed over the weekend vanished immediately when entering her office. Seated stiff and erect, in a leather chair offering no smile, no good morning greetings, sat Lorenzo's executioner. Without raising her head to face the doomed, she spoke, "A background check is required for all personnel." Lorenzo didn't hear what was said after that. He didn't need to. He knew the words letter-perfect-you're un-hirable.

Late that evening my cell phone rang and the instant we were connected I heard, "Max, I forgot about the background check being mandatory. I should've stayed part-time. Now I am out of work again." Silence and tears carried the moment. A long pause, then a whisper, I heard him praying, "Please help me, Lord. Please help me."

Paul writes in Philippians 4:11: "I have learned in whatever state I am, to be content." That doesn't mean we're to be all smiles when life's storms assail. Nevertheless, we can be confident that behind all outbursts of sufferings, God's fingerprints are found. Jeremiah 29:11 says, "I know the plans I have for you, says the LORD, plans of peace and not of evil, to give you a future and a hope."

As you examine your life, wondering how you measure up in the "poor in spirit" department, I offer a guideline through scripture.

I begin with Psalm 131:2: "Surely I have calmed and quieted my soul, like a weaned child with his mother; like a weaned child is my soul within me."

The word "soul" in this passage may be taken for desire. The psalmist has stilled and quieted his soul of his own desires. At last, he's finding contentment with God's plan rather than his own. That's huge for those with aspirations of savoring peace that passes all understanding. Often, however, we live life, as Acts 9:5 says, "Kicking against the goads." The metaphor is of an ox, in rebellion, driving the goad (prick) deeper by kicking against it. When we come against God's plan for our lives, we become the ox. Each time we throw a fit over our circumstances, we cause ourselves unnecessary mental anxiety. To be poor in spirit is to fall to our knees before God praying, "Lord, give me strength to cease fighting against Your will." That's to be poor in spirit.

2 Corinthians 3:18 says, "But we all, with unveiled face, beholding as in a mirror the glory of the Lord, are being transformed into the same image from glory to glory, just as by the Spirit of the Lord." Our part, by the power of the Holy Spirit, is to confess our need of Jesus Christ in everything in our lives. In so doing, blessed shall we be!

Chapter 3

Blessed are those who mourn,
for they shall be comforted.

—Matthew 5:4

A week before Thanksgiving, I found myself unsettled as I wandered through the living room, pausing long enough to gaze out the picture window at winter's bleakness. With our planned retirement trip a distant two months away, my imagination began to wander. Normally, my pessimistic side would've impulsively muttered reasons to nix any eccentric rationale. However, my positive side, abruptly and out of character, spoke up, Why not head for Florida, now? In a few years, you'll be requesting a bed pan from the night nurse. With that heartening or dis-heartening thought, I headed out to find my wife.

Once expressing my out of the box thinking to my wife, I attempted waiting patiently for a response. "Well, why not," I eagerly announced, "why not pack and leave?"

Her measured response was dead on. "Because you, Mr. King of back peddling, as soon as I entertain your craziness, you'll expeditiously recant of the whole idea."

Grinning, I began serenading her. "Not this time, sweet one, not this time." The following morning, we're south bound.

For the next three months we were on an emotional high, excited over experiencing life in a totally new way. It wasn't until the closing stages of our stay that I received a call from a childhood friend. Once answering his questions regarding my life, I returned the favor by asking about his life. The short version: he had a tumor removed from the brain. Inquiring how long he'd been home from the hospital, he replied, "Not home yet, calling from the hospital bed."

Without pausing, he continued, "Maxie (my neighborhood name he stuck me with), I've a favor to ask."

"This week, my younger brother, Jeff, underwent emergency brain surgery." Bringing up his brother's name stirred his raw emotions, and he paused to gather himself. "Would you talk to Jeff, you know, about the Lord? He'll listen to you, Maxie."

I have no recollection what he said after that, as I couldn't move past the striking scene of Harry grieving over his brother, while at death's door himself.

Harry never physically mended from the traumatic attempt by a team of surgeons to disconnect a cancerous tumor from the brain. Within months following surgery, Harry died. So in keeping with the promise I made to Harry regarding visiting his brother, who was back in the hospital, I went to see Jeff.

Once entering the hospital elevator, and pushing the button marked twelve, I leaned back against the wall, mentally picturing what to expect. Gnawing at me was the matter of Jeff's state of being. It wasn't unreal to visualize surgical tubes inserted in every opening of his body. This meant I could expect, at best, eye contact as his means of communication. Moreover, nibbling at my conscious was the idea I no longer was the person he once knew that didn't take a back seat to anyone when it came to living life with no restraints. Now, with "clergy" attached to my name, would he see me as phony, pretentious, fake, a hypocrite, or unauthentic? As for me, I felt I could enjoy Jeff as the person I've always known. My uncertainty was would Jeff see me in a similar manner? I would soon find out as the elevator bell pinged, signaling next stop, the twelfth floor.

Entering Jeff's room, he was observantly sitting up in bed, viewing the city from what he would later term as his "twelfth-floor penthouse". In no time, we launched into reminiscing our youthful years. His countenance blossomed as he dramatized stories that had me as the subject for the laughter. It felt good playing a part in Jeff's happiness.

After ten minutes of merriment, we settled down. It was then I inquired as to how he became aware of having a brain tumor. He leaned back into his pillow and for a few seconds gazed at the ceiling, seemingly pondering the question before him. Then turning his head in my direction, he commenced recounting his nightmare.

"I was home alone. Ann (his wife) was at work, and our youngest daughter, who'll be a senior, was out with friends. I was walking from the living room into the kitchen when abruptly both legs, simultaneously and instantly, ceased functioning. My forward motion threw me into the kitchen table like a wrecking ball and then onto the floor. At first, I thought I tripped. Face down on the floor, I mumbled something not worth repeating, then placing my hands on the floor as if to do push-ups, I attempted to pull my legs up under me. No movement whatsoever. Again, I mentally commanded my legs to move. Nothing. Instant fear, dissimilar to anything I ever experienced pounced on me."

Jeff paused for a brief second, again turning his eyes upward, seemingly searching for the courage to continue. I was readying myself to say, "Jeff, no need to go on," when he proceeded.

"Our pet dog, Hooper (Hoop for short), hearing the commotion, charged to the kitchen to investigate. Seeing me on the floor meant one thing to Hoop. Playtime. He turned and raced out of the kitchen only to return seconds later dragging his blanket. Normally, I'd get down on the floor and we'd play tug of war. However, I was in a war already and in no mood to play. Promptly becoming irritable, I pushed Hoop aside followed by a harsh, 'No'.

"I turned my focus to my legs that appeared similar to the flimsy legs of Scarecrow's in the Wizard of Oz. Mental assaults came fast and furious. I was dying. I was dying, and my family wasn't there to say goodbye. In between sobs, I weakly began mumbling, 'Please come home honey. Come home Jenny. Come home Sally. Come home Adam. Please someone come home'." Jeff concluded his emotional chronicle by telling of his daughter returning home, finding him on the floor and calling 9-1-1.

My allotted time to visit was coming to a close, yet I promised his brother I would raise up the name of Christ. However, as I wrote earlier, for years Jeff and I traveled the broader way that leads to destruction (Matthew 7:13). Now, years later, I stood before him as one saved through the death, burial, and resurrection of Jesus Christ. Would Jeff accept my transformation as genuine, allowing the prayer from his old friend to penetrate his heart?

I suddenly blurted out, "Jeff, I would like to pray with you before leaving." As I prayed, my words were soon accompanied by Jeff's emotional utterances. I want to believe that at that moment, heaven came down and glory filled the room and Jeff's heart.

In Romans 12:2, Paul spoke these words. "Do not be conformed to this world, but be transformed by the renewing of your mind." I read where it's one thing to point out a goal to a person and to encourage him to try to reach it. It's a different matter to show what should be done to reach that goal. Paul writes, "Stop allowing yourselves to be fashioned after the pattern of this evil age." The mind is the active ruling part of us, so that the renewing of the mind is the renewing of the whole man.

The first blessing Jesus makes possible through His death and resurrection is found in 1 John, 2:1–2. "My little children, these things I write to you, so that you may not sin. And if anyone sins, we have an Advocate with the Father, Jesus Christ the righteous. And He Himself is the propitiation for our sins." If not on guard, our minds envisage God's blessings as just pleasantries. Conversely, more times than not, God's sacred sign comes when hearts and minds embark on a soul journey of transformation brought on by regret. Romans 7:24 says, "O wretched man that I am! Who will deliver me from this body of death?" Embracing Paul's mindset as our own, blessed shall we be.

1 John 2:1–2 speaks of the blessing of all blessings. "We have an Advocate with the Father, Jesus Christ the righteous. And He Himself is the propitiation for our sins." The word propitiation means to appease or pacify. God the Son satisfied God the Father's decree found in Ezekiel 18:4: "Behold, all souls are mine; the souls of the father as well as the soul of the son is mine; the soul who sins shall die." Man has a date with death, and it's the spiritual dying rather

than the physical that should disquiet us most. To be pronounced guilty for rejecting Christ and His teachings is to face eternal hell, and for one who believes in a heaven and a hell, it's bleakness at the highest level. Romans 3:10 states, "There is no one righteous, no not one." Therefore, doomed are we without a means to eradicate our sinful follies.

The Bible joyfully proclaims the means by which sins can be exterminated as 1 Timothy elatedly points out in 2:5–6: "For there is one God and one Mediator between God and men, the Man Christ Jesus, who gave Himself a ransom for all." God invited Jesus to be man's only source of hope on the day of judgment. Scripture doesn't say Jesus, accompanied by man's good deeds, is the solution for appeasement with God. Ephesians points this out in 2:8–9: "For by grace you have been saved through faith, and that not of yourselves; it is the gift of God, not of works, lest anyone should boast."

Earlier I wrote of my friend grieving over his brother's sickness, not for the reason his brother's life on this earth was coming to an end. Rather, he mourned his brother's reluctance to repent. Acts 3:19 urges, "Repent therefore and be converted, that your sins may be blotted out, so that times of refreshing may come from the presence of the Lord." Times of refreshment are to be spiritually renewed through Christ, born again if you will, while remorseful by way of repentance for our sins against God.

I recall experiencing an unforgettable event in my adolescent years depicting regret. Study hall was the crime scene, a designated location where students studied in silence. My partner and I ignored the no talking rule until feeling a light tapping sensation on my shoulder. Without breaking the silence, the teacher motioned the two of us to follow him to the chalkboard. Once drawing two circles the size of softballs, he whispered, "Place your nose in the circle."

On tiptoes, face plastered against the chalkboard, I stretched and strained to place my nose inside the circle. Minutes later, my nose began sliding downward, out of the circle.

The teacher quietly moved up from behind and again whispered, "Need help?"

"Yes," I speedily replied.

With that, he stepped back and unleashed a wooden paddle against my backside. My nose immediately shot up to the uppermost part of the circle. Again, a soft whisper. "Is that enough help?"

Without hesitation and before a sizeable tear dropped to the floor, I slurred, "Yes."

I regretted whispering in study hall due to the consequences for my actions rather than out of respect for the teacher's rules. The question before us is how do we know when we're truly sorrowful over sins, or just sorrowful for getting caught?

At church revivals, I've observed what appeared to be people heartbroken over a wayward life. However, with passing of time, nothing changed in their continued sinful demeanor. I conclude that a pretentious display of emotions isn't the mourning Christ speaks of in the Beatitudes. 2 Corinthians 7:10 says, "For godly sorrow produces repentance leading to salvation." When remorsefulness comes from a regretful heart, blessed shall we be.

A Sunday school teacher asked her class to define repentance.

A little boy shot up his hand and replied, "Repentance means sorrow for being bad."

"Well done," said the teacher.

Now, little Becky, not to be outdone by Tommy Tucker, said, "Excuse me, teacher, it really means sorry enough to 'stop' being bad." To mourn our sin, like the little girl said, is to break from a lifestyle that doesn't honor God. The apostle Peter in Matthew 26:74–75 was confronted with the battle against his old nature. "Then he began to curse and swear, saying, 'I do not know the Man!' Immediately a rooster crowed. And Peter remembered the word of Jesus who had said to him, before the rooster crows, you will deny Me three times. With that, he went out and wept bitterly." Peter was angry, bemoaning his old sinful nature that, while it didn't reign over him, was alive and well. Hopefully, once recognizing this truth that applies to all believers, we can press on toward sanctification.

King David said in Psalm 38:18, "For I will declare my iniquity; I will be in anguish over my sin." Often, David underwent painful self-examinations, and it was extremely uncomfortable due to evaluating his life based on God's standards, not his neighbors. Remorse over falling back into our old nature, followed by repentance, is an ongoing exercise. That's the meaning of transformation, and for the person who participates in this continuous journey of change, blessed shall you be.

The Apostle Paul must have begun his Christian journey feeling positive about his spirituality. Galatians 1 opens with, "Paul, an apostle—not from men nor through man, but through Jesus Christ and God the Father." I dare say, Paul battled pride a time or two as he knew the prominence being a chosen vessel of God's. Who wouldn't feel special if Jesus were to speak vocally to us the way He spoke to Paul on the road to Damascus? As a result, Paul cried out in Acts 9:5, "'Who are You, Lord?' The Lord said, 'I am Jesus, whom you are persecuting'." As years passed, Paul became more and more conscious of his old former depravity. He writes in 1 Corinthians 15:9, "For I am the least of the apostles, who am not worthy to be called an apostle, because I persecuted the church of God." While humbly acknowledging his wonderful status, having been saved by grace, he was also mindful of his shortcomings. Keenly aware of the need of God's mercy, he declares in Ephesians 3:8, "To me, who am less than the least of all the saints, this grace was given, that I should preach among the Gentiles the unsearchable riches of Christ."

At the end of Paul's magnificent journey on earth, he writes in 1 Timothy 1:15, "This is a faithful saying and worthy of all acceptances, that Christ Jesus came into the world to save sinners, of whom I am chief." Mindful our bent-on sinning can be humbling while uplifting. First, awareness of our sin comes directly from the Holy Spirit within us. Secondly, when conscious of our depravity, it gives evidence of God being busy at work in our lives.

Jesus raised the spirits of those who courageously mourned their depravity that day on the Mount. "Blessed are those who mourn, for they shall be comforted." The above passage gives hope to those who petition God with a mournful heart. No matter what sincere sorrow we bring before our Creator, scripture promises we'll be welcomed and blessed. It's essential to understand forgiveness comes where there is regret over our, at times, wayward life. The reason being people grieve for countless reasons.

For example, my wife and I mourned our pet's death. I recall the vet's initial words upon hearing our dog's coughing. "She has heartworms, and there's nothing to prescribe that will prolong the inevitable." Cradling her in my arms, master and friend resigned to the inevitable. A kiss on her forehead, followed by a few personal words, our journeying together came to its end. My wife waited at home, stationing herself by the picture window. Returning without Chuckles said all that needed said, and in one another's arms, we mourned the death of our pet.

Then there's bereavement over wounded pride. My hometown had two junior high schools, each housing seventh through ninth grades, located at opposite ends of the city. Nonetheless, the two schools combined their ninth-grade sports programs, creating one freshmen team. Tryouts were required for making the roster. The first evaluation was to see who was blessed with speed. When the coach barked, "On your mark, get set, go," I exploded off the line, but instead of striding forward, I did a nose dive, and with that the coach quickly blew the whistle. Picking myself up while removing gravel from a bleeding snout, we were ordered to line up again. "On your mark, get set, go!" Again, I experienced gravel hitting my face. However, this time, it wasn't from falling. It was due to being in last place and getting pelted from the competition kicking up gravel. With that, my football career bit the dust.

Believing I fit in somewhere in freshmen sports, I tried track and field. From my experience in football tryouts, I knew I wasn't a speedster, so I'd give the long jump a go. I recall running down the runway toward the sand pit and then leaping into the air. I felt as though I was soaring, and if correct, high marks were soon to follow. With my butt planted in the sand, I turned to look back to where I began. Talk about disappointment. Then, attempting to stand, my calf muscle cramped. There I am, rolling in the sand, squealing like a wounded pig. And wouldn't you know it, the boy who beat me out in football was witnessing my grand performance. Moving into the pit, he offered his hand, pulling me to my feet. My self-esteem, self-worth, and shame all joined in on the grieving.

Next comes inappropriate mourning. In 2 Samuel 13, Ammon mourned being denied sex with his own sister. He may have fabricated sickness in order to get his sister at his bedside, but there was no pretention regarding his mental illness.

Fabricating mourning is again found in 1 Kings 21. Ahab was denied a plot of land, and he sorrowed to the point he crawled into bed, threatening never to get out. His pathetic grieving is seen in verses 2–5: "'Give me your vineyard, that I may have it for a vegetable garden, because it is near, next to my house; and for it I will give you a vineyard better than it. Or, if it seems good to you, I will give you its worth in money.' But Naboth said to Ahab, 'The LORD forbid that I should give the inheritance of my fathers to you!' So Ahab went into his house sullen and displeased because of the word which Naboth the Jezreelite had spoken to him; for he had said, 'I will not give you the inheritance of my fathers.' And he lay down on his bed, and turned away his face, and would eat no food." The only thing missing was for Ahab to begin sucking his thumb. Illicit sorrow is when a person mourns externally while the heart never sheds a tear.

The sorrow Jesus refers to on Mount Sinai is a heartfelt grieving over blatantly ignoring God's commands. The person who genuinely mourns their sin will be uplifted by God. Reading Psalm 51:17: "The sacrifices of God are a broken spirit, A broken and a contrite heart—These, O God, You will not despise."

I close with teachings from John 14:16: "And I will pray the Father, and He will give you another Helper, that He may abide with you forever, the Spirit of truth." Those who genuinely mourn their sin will most certainly be blessed.

Chapter 4

Blessed Are the Meek for They Shall Inherit the Earth

—Matthew 5:5

In 2011, an analyst of college basketball's March madness reported defeated teams were beaten in numerous ways: weren't strong in rebounding, weak when it came to blocking out, or lacked aggressiveness. Victory in the sporting arena seldom comes through meekness. However, playing the game of life outside the sporting arena, Jesus teaches real strength is exhibited through submissiveness. In order to witness this truth in action, join me on the sideline to observe a few of yesteryear's followers of God triumphing through meekness.

For three hundred years after Noah built the ark, God remained silent until Genesis 12:1. "Now the Lord had said to Abram: Get out of your country, from your family and from your father's house, to a land that I will show you." Up until that time, Abram previously moved only once. However, this move was under God's directive, designed both to try Abram's faith and separate him from his country's idolatrous lifestyle. With the exception of his nephew and his clan, no other was invited to join Abram in the journey.

Genesis 13:1 says, "So Abram departed as the Lord had instructed, accompanied by his nephew Lot and his clan." At first, Abram thought it a good idea having family accompany him on his new adventure. However, following a prolonged period of togetherness, the caravan unraveled. Genesis 13: 6–7 says, "Now the land was not able to support them that they might dwell together, for their possessions were so great that they could not dwell together. And there was strife between the herdsmen of Abram's livestock and the herdsmen of Lot's livestock."

Abram and his nephew acquired masses of wealth as seen by their very significant holdings of livestock. Which meant their livestock required sizeable amounts of pasture land. It's at this point Abram could have caused a sizeable stir as his nephew, so to speak, was just along for the ride. Nonetheless, rather than exercise his position of authority, Abram demonstrated power through meekness. Genesis 13:8–9 says, "So Abram said to Lot, 'Please let there be no strife between you and me, and between my herdsmen and your herdsmen; for we are brethren. Is not the whole land before you? Please separate from me. If you take the left, then I will go to the right; or, if you go to the right, then I will go to the left'." It's here; Abram's authority is heightened through humbleness.

Identical to Abram and Lot's journeying, believers traveling alongside nonbelievers are given opportunities to display God's presence and beauty through humility. Philippians 2:3–4 says, "Let nothing be done through selfish ambition or conceit, but in lowliness of mind let each esteem others better than himself. Let each of you look out not only for his interests, but also for the interests of others." Abram understood life to be more than chasing dreams of prosperity, fool's gold if you will. It was a violation of his life's purpose while on earth to seek fulfillment in anything other than God.

Abram's meekness wasn't weakness irrespective of what Richard Dawkins, the self-proclaimed atheist, actively proclaims. Dawkins is sarcastically amused at the so-called Christian community requiring help and power from outside themselves to live out life. In his nonbelief of a moral law giver, an eternal living God, he sees a dependency on such beliefs as nothing but weakness. Abram was far removed from Dawkins' thinking. While Lot quickly selected the choicest pastures, Abram meekly, not weakly, but confidently relied on God's instruction.

King David

When investigating King David's life experiences, what's unexpected is his compassionate heart. I'm cautious writing that, for in 1

Samuel 18:6, it says, "Now it had happened as they were coming home, when David was returning from the slaughter." Unquestionably, David wasn't to be messed with, even as a kid. Caring for his father's flock, he displayed the resolve to stand his ground. 1 Samuel 17:34 says, "Your servant used to keep his father's sheep and when a lion or a bear came and took a lamb out of the flock I went out after it and struck it, and delivered the lamb from its mouth; and when it arose against me, I caught it by its beard, and struck and killed it. Your servant has killed both lion and bear."

David stood toe to toe with Goliath who measured nine feet tall with strength to match. From David's prospective, Goliath, dressed in protective armor weighing one hundred pounds plus, must've resembled something out of Star Wars. Our being witnesses that day, we would've heard David's emotions escalating as he yelled out in 1 Samuel 17: 47, "all this assembly shall know that the LORD does not save with sword and spear; for the battle is the LORD's, and He will give you into our hand."

David continued to be victorious on the battlefield, and through being triumphant, he became the people's choice. The ladies of the community composed a ditty honoring David in 1 Samuel 1:7, "Saul has slain his thousands, and David his ten thousands." However, with all that is written about King David's might, his most celebrated victories came through his heart, not his hands.

Meekness separated him above and beyond the standard measurement of men. In 1 Samuel 24, David is running for his life. King Saul was sick and tired of David's accomplishments overshadowing his own, and Saul was determined to end this nuisance by taking David's life. During the exhausting manhunt, King Saul pauses long enough to enter a cave, tending to physical necessities. No coincidence David was hiding in the exact cavern. In 1 Samuel 24:4, David's men were beside themselves, whispering to David, "This is the day of which the LORD said to you, 'Behold, I will deliver your enemy into your hand, that you may do to him as it seems good to you'." David, however, had no intention of harming Saul, for to David, the king was God's chosen one. No amount of pressure from those around him would've persuaded David to lay a hand on God's anointed.

SHOWERS OF BLESSINGS

Before continuing, allow me to give an illustration of what meekness doesn't look like. Our one and only vehicle at the time was under repair. I borrowed a family member's automobile for a few days, and when the few days passed, we were approached on when the vehicle would be returned. Those words hit me like a bee sting. What smarted was my pride. It was a "how dare they" sort of thing. There wasn't a morsel, a tad, or a scrap of meekness displayed on my part. Soiled words were vocalized, feelings were hurt, and regret accompanied me to bed. Therefore, as I continue on, know for sure, this message speaks to yours truly.

In 2 Samuel 16:6, we find David again in a forced flight from Jerusalem. This time, he's running from his son, Absalom, who was attempting to overthrow his father's kingship. Absalom wanted nothing to do with being a successor, inheritor, or an heir. Being a beneficiary meant waiting, and he certainly wasn't hanging around for his time to come. Absalom coveted the position of power, and he coveted it "now." If to acquire dominance meant destroying his father, so be it. To make matters worse, in David's attempt to avoid his obsessed offspring, he enters a village that doesn't have a welcome mat out for his arrival. He runs into Shimei who is related to none other than Saul. If David was to remain king, Shimei stood no chance of getting a seat of power. For a time, Shimei kept to himself his feelings regarding David. However, now that David is on the run and David's kingship is up for grabs, Shimei was free to vent, and vent he did. Hurling stones along with profane words, Shimei had been sitting on stored up anger, and now it exploded.

David was in a position to declare, "Enough is enough. First my son, now this madman goes off on me. Pin him to the ground with a spear." In fact, David's bodyguards were biting at the bit to do just that. However, David's meekness forbade his accusers blood to be spilled. At the end of Shimei's unrelenting attack, David responds in 2 Samuel 16:11, "And David said to Abishai and all his servants, See how my son who came from my own body seeks my life. How much more now may this Benjamite? Let him alone, and let him curse; for so the LORD has ordered him." Meekness is anything but weakness, and unfortunately, it's a strength few have noticeably refined.

Later, while fleeing from King Saul, traumatic news reaches David. Absalom, David's prodigal son, was killed in battle. David's response is found in 2 Samuel 18:33, "Then the king was deeply moved, and went up to the chamber over the gate, and wept. And as he went, he said thus: "O my son Absalom—my son, my son Absalom—if only I had died in your place! O Absalom my son, my son." Meekness always rises above vanity.

Joseph

In Genesis 37, we read of the erosion of a relationship between Joseph and his brothers. Well recognized in Jacob's family, little brother Joseph, was the apple of their father's eye. If that wasn't enough to bring about resentment, Joseph was a dreamer, finding great delight retelling his visions to his brothers. Genesis 37:5-7: "Now Joseph had a dream, and he told it to his brothers; and they hated him even more. So he said to them, 'Please hear this dream which I have dreamed: There we were, binding sheaves in the field. Then behold, my sheaf arose and also stood upright; and indeed your sheaves stood all around and bowed down to my sheaf.' Apparently at the time, Joseph, lacking common sense, failed to recognize his brother's deep-seated resentment oozing out. Nonetheless, Joseph was on a roll as another fancy danced like a sugar plum in his head. Genesis 37:9: "Then he dreamed still another dream and told it to his brothers, and said, 'Look, I have dreamed another dream. And this time, the sun, the moon, and the eleven stars bowed down to me'." As you well realize by now, Joseph isn't practicing meekness, but he'll get there following years of great heartache.

To appreciate his brother's mind-set upon hearing Joseph's visions, people in antiquity were greatly affected by dreams. They would've questioned if Joseph's fantasy might possibly have been communicated from the unseen world. The thought of giving homage to Joseph in the future brought about what follows.

Time came when Jacob's sons, with the exception of Joseph, were away watching over the family's sheep herd in Shechem, miles from their home in Hebron. Due to the distance, Jacob sent Joseph to check on the well-being of his sons. Prior to Joseph's arrival, the brothers were in a heated conversation regarding the spoiled brat. Genesis 37:18: "Now when they saw him afar off, even before he came near them, they conspired against him to kill him." Proverbs 14:30 says, "A sound heart is life to the body, but envy is rottenness to the bonds."

Genesis 37:23–24 says, "So it came to pass, when Joseph had come to his brothers, that they stripped Joseph of his tunic, the tunic of many colors that was on him. Then they took him and cast him into a pit. And the pit was empty; there was no water in it." Mission accomplished, or so they thought. A tormented conscious caused the brothers to quietly pick at the evening meal. Scripture is silent concerning the elapsed time before a caravan was spotted. What we do know is the convoy was a welcomed sight to their guilt as seen in Genesis 37:27. "Come and let us sell him to the Ishmaelites, and let not our hand be upon him, for he is our brother and our flesh." Pulling Joseph from the well resembled Jesus calling Lazarus from the tomb. He was good as dead until the arrival of the caravan. Joseph's emotions must have flip-flopped many times. Forced to leave family and friends felt like death. Nonetheless, being brought back from the dead made it most difficult not to have feelings of thanksgiving.

Despite being shackled, Joseph had a new lease on life. Potiphar, a high-ranking officer of Pharaoh, purchased Joseph from the Ishmaelite traders. Potiphar's investment in Joseph paid huge dividends resembling the blessings Moses spoke of in Deuteronomy 28. "Blessed shall you be in the city, and blessed shall you be in the country." Joseph was quickly elevated to chief steward of Potiphar's household.

The saying, "nothing stays the same," was an absolute for Joseph's life. His position of prominence came crashing in when he snubbed his boss's wife's sexual advances. Crushed pride sent her sobbing to her hubby. Scripture is uncommunicative regarding whether or not Joseph vehemently attempted to defend himself against these false charges of misconduct. What we do know is that Joseph placed his life unreservedly into God's care. Joseph kept before him a mindset attested to in Acts 24:16. "This being so, I myself always strive to have a conscience without offense toward God and men." I'll skip Joseph's stretch in the dungeon to get to when providence brings Joseph face-to-face with his brothers.

Shortly after Joseph's release from the dungeon, he resumed his duties as chief aid to Pharaoh. During that time Joseph was called upon to interpret the dream of the King. His interpretation revealed that in seven years there would be a severe famine in all the land. Pharaoh, trusting Joseph's discernment, placed him in charge of storing up grain and supplies throughout those years. The day came when Joseph had the opportunity for a vengeful payback party.

Twenty years passed since Joseph last spoke to any of his clan. In those years, Jacob's sons married and were raising families of their own. Nevertheless, they were incorporated into one society under the presidency of their father, Jacob. Subsequently, when the land of Canaan suffered under a famine, Jacob instructed his sons to travel to Egypt to purchase grain. Little did they know, the dreams which Joseph shared with them were soon to become real.

The story is now fast-forwarded to when the brothers are in Egypt, standing before Joseph, whom they didn't recognize. It's Joseph having the upper hand with several options: reject their request for food, lock them up not for days, but years, or worse. Nonetheless, Joseph understood benevolence like never before. Upon hearing Reuben's words in 42:22, "Did I not speak to you, saying, 'Do not sin against the boy'; and you would not listen? Therefore behold, his blood is now required of us," Joseph turned himself away from them and wept. His affection came pouring out, displaying a heart filled with meekness. An amazing reuniting came about through Joseph living life through true humility not power. The ending is in Genesis 45:14–15, "Then he fell on his brother Benjamin's neck and wept, and Benjamin wept on his neck. Moreover, he kissed all his brothers and wept over them, and after that his brothers talked with him."

Meekness is strength when possessing the power to chide, crush, or rebuke, but opts for tenderness. How we respond when wronged articulates where we are in our journey of loving and following the Lord's teachings.

Jesus

Jesus is our final subject for witnessing how meekness is lived out in its most excellent way. In Isaiah 53:7, it says, "He was oppressed and He was afflicted, Yet He opened not His mouth; He was led as a lamb to the slaughter, and as a sheep before its shearers is silent, so He opened not His mouth."

Believers are known to behave out of character when stressed. Such an occasion might have occurred during the week of Jesus's crucifixion, as God the Father, an eyewitness to what the goons were doing to His Son, remained neutral and silent. The magazine, National Geographic, has enlarged city folks understanding on the temperament of sheep during shearing. Rather than becoming aggressive, they convert to meekness and submissiveness. It's with that temperament Isaiah describes Jesus journey to the cross.

When the infuriated crowd pelted Jesus with false accusations, I've often thought about the moment when an officer struck Jesus. John 18:22 says it this way: "And when He had said these things, one of the officers who stood by struck Jesus with the palm of his hand, saying, 'Do You answer the high priest like that?'" If Jesus doesn't practice meekness, the officer is dead along with our salvation. Tormented, He made no threat to His tormentor, such as, "You'll get yours". Rather, 1 Peter 2:23 explains exactly how Jesus responded. "When He was reviled, did not revile in return; when He suffered, He did not threaten, but committed Himself to Him who judges righteously."

Living a life of meekness in the fashion Jesus displayed requires strength not found in man's makeup. Left to ourselves, its pie in the sky thinking to believe we can be victorious over Satan and self when left without the strength from above. Such fortitude requires a force beyond our capacity to achieve. The psalmist's words guide us into hope when under despair. "But those who wait on the Lord, they shall inherit the earth. For yet a little while and the wicked shall be no more; indeed, you will look carefully for his place, but it shall be no more. But the meek shall inherit the earth, and shall delight themselves in the abundance of peace (Psalm 37:9–11).

Psalm 37 places us on the right path for living a life of meekness. Verse 3 starts off with, "Trust in the Lord". I'll be first to confess it's a struggle relying on God rather than circumstances. Nevertheless, solely through the power of the Holy Spirit can we ever hope to honor God by entrusting life experiences, be they good or grave, into Jesus' wonderful care.

Verse 4 builds off of verse 3: "Delight yourself in the Lord." Delighting in God is placing our confidence in God no matter what we're faced with.

Verse 5 reminds us of our responsibility. "Commit your way to the Lord, and Trust also in Him." Vacate whatever is torpedoing your hopes, which often is self. Impatience can sink a mind-set that is moving toward honoring God.

And the ending is verse 7: "Rest in the Lord." Cease from fretting is a huge as well as a monumental challenge. Nevertheless, 1 John 5:4 offers hope: "For whatever is born of God overcomes the world. And this is the victory that has overcome the world—our faith." Not ourselves having a certain amount of faith, rather, who we have our faith in. Where we place our hope determines the amount of peace we enjoy when our world is falling asunder.

Jesus being triumphant in all his undertakings makes possible our succeeding in living out life through meekness. Philippians 1:6 says, "being confident of this very thing, that He who has begun a good work in you will complete it until the day of Jesus Christ." For the very reason that our confidence is not with ourselves, but with Christ, is the encouragement we need to press on. A meek lifestyle is most certainly attainable. Philippians 3:12 says, "Not that I have already attained, or am already perfected; but I press on, that I may lay hold of that for which Christ Jesus has also laid hold of me."

The phrase "pressing on" implies that there are trials ahead. Meekness doesn't come by traveling on the yellow brick road. On the contrary, meekness is developed through grueling seasons of painful run-throughs. Nevertheless, our living life in humility is one of the promises for which Jesus died.

Developing a personality of meekness

Galatians 5:23 says, "But the fruit of the Spirit is love, joy, peace, longsuffering, kindness, goodness, faithfulness, gentleness, self-control. Against such there is no law. And those who are Christ's have crucified the flesh with its passions and desires." Exactly how does a person absorb into one's soul the fruits of the Spirit while putting to death the fleshly passion of human cravings? Know for sure, it doesn't come simply by way of strong willpower. We smile and speak kindly to others, while our old nature may be seething with disdain. Which is to say, meekness isn't manufactured or force-fed. It comes by spending time with God.

Chapter 5

Blessed Are Those Who Hunger and Thirst for
Righteousness, for They Shall Be Filled

—Matthew 5:6

What's your thirst?

The war in Vietnam showed no signs of tapering off, and although President Nixon proclaimed victory, the military knew better. The draft was implemented, and I found myself stationed at Fort Polk, Louisiana, training for jungle warfare. Unlike the actual bloody combat that was taking place in Southeast Asia, at the Fort, we played war. Nonetheless, through field training, we knew GIs experienced, if just a taste, the strain combat personnel lived with constantly while in harm's way.

Louisiana, known for subtropical climates, was in a deep drought with temperatures climbing into triple digits, crafting a Vietnam war zone atmosphere.

Field exercises took place where striped bark scorpions, water moccasins, and gators called home. Adding to that stress was the hassle of repeatedly setting up and tearing down a camp two and three times a day. With insignificant pocket-sized moments for snoozing, attitudes rapidly wilted. However, what was on the rise was negligence. Failure to replenish the water canteen each morning was to break the first rule in a desert like climate.

As always, before daybreak, we hurriedly broke camp, resuming the dreaded push through tangled terrain. By midmorning, when the heat index was over the top, I discovered the inconceivable—my canteen was bone dry. Snakes, scorpions, lions, tigers, bears, alligators, and the rest of the animal kingdom no longer consumed my thinking. It was water on the rocks.

Weary from tramping, crawling, and cutting through underbrush the better part of an afternoon, my partner came to a halt. In no mood for conversation, he pulled out his compass, took a reading and then shoved the scope into my chest. He wasn't taking another step until the two of us were like-minded on the direction we were headed. The heat and abhorrence of being drafted into this hell hole he was forced into had him on the verge of cracking. Impatiently, he eyeballed me until he didn't have it in him to wait one second more. "Well," he harshly blurted out, "are we on course?"

Raising my head from studying the compass, I looked squarely into his face and declared, "Can I have a drink from your canteen?" No need to give you a blow by blow how he responded to that statement.

Having a deep thirst for something dictates how one thinks and acts throughout life. Mankind's number one longing is happiness, and he'll chase that elusiveness right up to facing death's door. Jeremiah 2:13 says, "For My people have committed two evils: They have forsaken Me, the fountain of living waters, and hewn themselves cisterns—broken cisterns that can hold no water." In Isaiah 55:2, the prophet wonders why. "Why do you spend money for what is not bread, and your wages for what does not satisfy?" What Isaiah proclaimed in the Old Testament Jesus declared on "Mount Beatitude". Fulfillment comes by way of embracing Christ Jesus as Savior while following His directives for living out life.

Christ's message on the mount pointed to meekness, brokenness, hungering, and thirsting for Christ as the means for attaining inner peace. As my thirst was satisfied drinking water from the canteen, Jesus promises the same through embracing God's offer for salvation. Deuteronomy 2:7 speaks of lacking nothing with God. "For the LORD your God has blessed you in all the work of your hand. He knows your trudging through this great wilderness. These forty years the LORD your God has been with you; you have lacked nothing."

The Lord stood watch over Israel forty years while they wandered in quest for happiness and serenity. There wasn't then, nor today, an experience that'll satisfy one's dehydrated soul other than the nourishment of fully encountering Christ.

Now we come to John 4:14: "but whoever drinks of the water that I shall give him will never thirst. But the water that I shall give him will become in him a fountain of water springing up into everlasting life." I paraphrase John's words by saying, once the spiritual palate, the soul, savors Jesus, thirst for fulfillment is appeased. However, much like when I returned to my buddies' canteen throughout the day, the believer will desire more and more of Christ.

In Exodus 14:16, God commands Moses, "Lift up your rod, and stretch out your hand over the sea and divide it. And the children of Israel shall go on dry ground through the midst of the sea." Later, in verse 26, the Lord said to Moses, "Stretch out your hand over the sea that the waters may come back upon the Egyptians." Moses was given a front row seat in beholding God's grandeur. If ever a person should have been completely satisfied by God's manifestations, Moses was that person.

However, in Exodus 33:18, Moses sums up what I'm driving at. "And he said, 'Please, show me your glory'." Moses's urgent plea was for God to put on display, again, God's magnificent glory. His plea parallels that of our children in their toddler years when we acted out bedtime stories. At the end of the drama, my audience, who were tucked in tight, would hullabaloo for more, "Do it again, Daddy. Please, Mommy, do it again." The children (and Mom and Dad) never tired of bedtime play, nor did Moses tire of beholding God's splendor. The reason makes perfect sense. With each experience Moses encountered with God, his confidence in the almighty matured. The story below fits well with how Moses's reliance on God evolved.

A little girl, like children do from time to time, asked her father a deep question. "Dad, what is the size of God?"

At first, he was taken back from his daughter's enquiry. Then the father looked up at the sky and pointed to a plane flying overhead and ask, how big is that plane? The great distance had the plane appearing tiny. The little girl replied, "Small, I can hardly see it."

The next day, the father and daughter visited a large airport. Getting reasonably close to a commercial plane, the father asked, "Now, how big is this plane?"

The little girl exclaimed, "Wow, it's huge!"

The same applies with God. The size of God depends on how close or far away you are to Him. The closer you are, the greater God will be in your life!

For Moses, each encounter with God brought about a craving for more of the same. A, "do it again daddy," sort of thing.

One thing more before parting company with the great patriarch of the past. At his death, it was God performing all functions of Moses's funeral. From planning his funeral, to embalmment, to pallbearers, to entombment and finally, to seeing over the guest list, which was made up of the heavenly host.

King David

David frequently witnessed God's providence, and the more God revealed His brilliance, the more David aspired to do His will. Psalm 42:1 says, "As the deer pants for the water brooks, so pants my soul for You, O God. My soul thirsts for God, for the living God." In periods of spiritual famine, David habitually called to mind occurrences of God's protection and involvement in his life.

I recall a Lay's Potato Chips commercial saying, "Bet you can't eat just one!" Once Lays chips enter the mouth and the taste buds break out into a happy dance, the eater will reach for another. That's the appetite David developed for God. Psalm 34:8 says, "Oh, taste and see that the LORD is good; Blessed is the man who trusts in Him!" Once relishing God's hands in His approach to our lives, we'll petition for more.

Psalm 63:1–2 go right along with this, "O God, You are my God; Early will I seek You; My soul thirsts for You; My flesh longs for You in a dry and thirsty land Where there is no water. So I have looked for You in the sanctuary, to see Your power and Your glory." Again, in Matthew 5:6, "Those who thirst for God will be filled." Not may be filled, or hopefully to be filled, but "filled". The question that must be answered is, filled with what? When I say filled with righteousness, the critic points to God's word in Romans 3:10: "There is none righteous, no, not one." Left to ourselves, it's futile to think of attaining righteousness. However, to the person who embraces Jesus as Savior, Christ imputes His righteousness into that person at that moment. Now, don't miss this next statement. The believer's nature doesn't become sinless the moment Christ enters. Nonetheless, when Christ imputes His righteousness into the soul of man, God sees the blood of His Son, covering the believer's past, present, and future sins. From God's prospective, although sin will show its ugly face from time to time, that person is credited as righteous.

Romans 5:9–11 put it this way, "Much more then, having now been justified by His blood, we shall be saved from wrath through Him. For if when we were enemies we were reconciled to God through the death of His Son, much more, having been reconciled, we shall be saved by His life. And not only that, but we also rejoice in God through our Lord Jesus Christ, through whom we have now received the reconciliation." The believer, through Jesus Christ, goes from being in conflict with God to peace and friendship. Having peace with the One who determines where eternal life is spent takes ones breath away.

An illustration may assist in driving home the joy of being filled with the living hope of Jesus Christ. I expounded on a message entitled, "The Depth of God's Love." The week leading up to Sunday's worship wasn't without disturbances bumping into one another. Monday morning kicked off with a call from the automotive repair business. Our one and only vehicle was struggling mechanically. The caller notifies us that the slight pause in the car's acceleration, when the gas pedal was pressed, was due to a sick transmission. The slight pause turned into a large $$ headache. The ditty that ran through my head as I hung up the phone was of the sixties. It was by the Mommas and the Papas, titled, "Monday, Monday". The lyrics go as follows:

> Monday, Monday
> can't trust that day.
> Monday, Monday sometimes it just turns out that way.

SHOWERS OF BLESSINGS

Every other day, every other day, every other day of the week is fine.
But whenever Monday comes, whenever Monday comes.
You find me crying all the time.

    Monday morning's ditty moved into Saturday night. The result of backed up water from a clogged sewer line, which spewed out all sorts of things in the bathroom. Helplessly, I stood gawking as stuff of all shapes and sizes floated at my feet. And of course, that weekend, we entertained out of town guests staying overnight. Living within minutes of the State Park, and the bathroom out of order, I exhibit hospitality by transporting our guest to the park's restrooms throughout the night.

    It's now Sunday morning, and although weary from running the night shuttle, I zip into the church's parking lot with not a minute to spare. While hurriedly making my way to the podium, I became distracted by the large wooden cross hanging on the front wall. I'd seen this Christian symbol hundreds of times; however, it was as though a veil covering my mind was pulled away, allowing the cross's truth to penetrate deeper still. I paused, then turned and faced the congregation. At a snail's tempo, my eyes leisurely moved and looked into faces of people seeking hope. They, like myself, needed to taste "again" the living God.

    The majority were well acquainted with suffering. There was Terry, sitting bent over in a section near the rear door. He'd been injured from a steel beam falling at his place of work, pinning him to the factory floor. Through the years, Terry's injury brought on multiple physical complications and his latest diagnosis—five years to live.

    Kim, on the other hand, sitting more toward the center, carried a different burden. Hers was mental anguish. Her damage came by way of a marriage torn asunder. A few years past, she sat beside the one who proclaimed on their wedding day to be the love of his life. Today, she sits deserted, numb, and alone.

    Nearer the front, snuggled up to Mommy, was a solemn seven-year-old by the name Tammy. She failed miserably attempting to conceal her aching heart. Her parent's divorced, and although Daddy moved to another town, he promised to visit weekly. After three months, Daddy has yet to be seen. He phones weekly, promising to come, yet something always prevents him from following through on his promise.

As I stood there looking out at the congregation, silence filled the sanctuary unlike anything I'd witnessed in years. Hesitant to disrupt the silence, I slowly turned my head back to the other side of the sanctuary before speaking. "God allows pain to enter our lives recurrently for a deeper reason than we humans can comprehend. Furthermore, scripture points to God as allowing, even directing sufferings." I then opened the Bible and read 1 Peter 1:6–7: "In this you greatly rejoice, though now for a little while, if need be, you have been grieved by various trials, that the genuineness of your faith, being much more precious than gold that perishes, though it is tested by fire, may be found to praise, honor, and glory at the revelation of Jesus Christ." So where is this peace that resembles a slow-moving river to be found? If God plays a part in our suffering, from where comes our peace?

The psalmist points in the opposite direction from where the world searches for fulfillment and healing. Psalm 34:8 says, "Oh, taste and see that the LORD is good." Suffering plays a massive part in directing us into the protective and healing arms of Jesus. It's in those dark times of our lives that the taste of God becomes more pronounced. Through tasting, which is taking God seriously, we'll cry out like Moses, "Lord, show me your glory, again."

Chapter 6

Blessed Are the Merciful, for
They Shall Obtain Mercy

—Matthew 5:7

One description of mercy is displaying kindness beyond what a person deserves. It's more than an emotion, it's an undertaking. For mercy to be given, one must have the power to express such an act of kindness. The following is an illustration of having the power to give or disallow generosity.

Throughout the night, silent fallen snow blanketed the landscape, transforming the countryside into a winter wonderland. Winter mornings were Erik's favorite time to walk the trails of a local state park. One footpath in particular orbited a miniature island with thick bushes lining the shoreline.

On one particular walk, Erik approached the far end of the island when something caught his attention at the water's edge. Peering through the scrubs, he encountered birds of some sort standing on the ice. He thought it a bit strange his presence didn't cause the birds to abruptly go airborne. Pushing the snow-covered limbs aside for a better look, he discovered a covey of coots staring at him. No frantic scurrying to flee his presence, they merely stood still as a stick, motionless as decoys. Caught by surprise, he stared back until realizing the unimaginable, the coots webbed fan-shaped feet were frozen to the ice. They chose to do an un-nature-like thing by resting for the night upon slushy ice. As nightfall closed in, temperatures plummeted cementing their feet to the frozen lake surface.

For the longest time, Erik simply gawked at the unusual sight. Once regaining his mental bearings, he pondered what action to take, if any. He knew choosing to help would most certainty come with a price. To start with, the coots were out of reach from where he stood. If he was to attempt a rescue mission, onto the ice he must step. Although Erik surmised the water wouldn't go over his boot tops, he toiled making up his mind. Countless times he moved forward to the ice edge, then backed off, to the edge, then backed off. In frustration he gave himself a dressing-down, "It's just ankle-deep water, do it."

Immediately stepping onto the ice, he plunged through. However, his calculation of the water's depth was a bit off. Instead of ankle deep, it was up to his knees. A moment of self-chastisement, then he stepped back onto the shore. Now what? Does he forget the rescue operation or wade in with both feet? He had the power to do either, which way would he go?

Before continuing with the illustration of what constitutes a form of mercy, I pause to talk on how mercy works when dealing with people. Granting kindness to someone who's caused us pain is no stress-free task. Pride says stand your ground. On the other hand, swallowing self-importance, which is a mouth full, is a huge price to pay if pride is to be defeated. Furthermore, denying the temptation to retaliate is a battle all on its own. The only way to display mercy is having the power to retaliate, yet choosing forgiveness. 1 John 1:6–7 says, "If we say that we have fellowship with Him, and walk in darkness, we lie and do not practice the truth. But if we walk in the light as He is in the light, we have fellowship with one another, and the blood of Jesus Christ His Son cleanses us from all sin." Pride hinders blessings; however, if living as scripture commands, God promises rivers in the desert. Joy may not come the moment mercy giving is extended, yet Psalm 27:14 says, "Wait on the LORD; be of good courage, And He shall strengthen your heart; Wait, I say, on the LORD!"

Back to bird watching. Erik was determined to free the trapped helpless coots, so back on and through the ice he went. Straddling the first coot, he placed both hands gently around the duck's fragile body and lightly lifted. Stuck. Attempting to jerk their legs loose would likely cause injury, the very thing he was attempting to prevent. With that, he stepped back onto land, sloshing his way back to the car. Returning home, he grabbed a chisel, a cardboard box, and within an hour was back at his rescue adventure. Once standing in ice water "again," he chipped around the miniscule webbed feet, until all fifteen were unstuck. Nonetheless, they weren't home free as their webbed feet resembled tiny ice anchors. For liberation to be complete, a meltdown was required if they were to fly. Into the cardboard box they went. Destination: furnace room.

Following the meltdown, the box containing Erik's precious cargo was carried outside. Once the lid was pulled back, all fifteen birds frantically headed skyward. From Erik's perspective, the coots thanked him by making a 360-degree flyover before heading back into the wild.

An extremely wholesome feeling came over him. It was the aftereffect of displaying mercy. It all began with having second thoughts. Was it worth wading in winter's glacial water to extend mercy to a few ill-fated ducks? Yes, for mercy wins out every time. Jesus said to those at Mount Beatitude, "Blessed are the merciful, for they shall obtain mercy." I paraphrase Jesus's words by saying blessings by God are sure to come to the merciful who have the power to retaliate when hurt by others, choose mercy instead.

In the gospel of Mark is a passage telling of cruel and merciless attacks on Jesus. Mark 14:65 says, "Then some began to spit on Him, and to blindfold Him, and to beat Him, and to say to Him, 'Prophesy!' And the officers struck Him with the palms of their hands." Jesus may well have terminated the torment before a hand ever touched His face. Nonetheless, Christ's nonviolent response reveals power, not weakness, which was the perfect display of what mercy looks like. Lamentation 3:22 says, "Through the LORD's mercies we are not consumed."

Dear reader, left to ourselves, there's no way we have strength to duplicate Jesus's compassion. However, living life through the strength of the Holy Spirit, mercy giving becomes a genuine possibility. Jesus's words in Acts 1:8 speak of being given strength to deny one's need to retaliate. "You shall receive power when the Holy Spirit has come upon you; and you shall be witnesses to Me in Jerusalem, and in all Judea and Samaria, and to the end of the earth." Whenever we, through the sovereignty of the Holy Spirit, defeat the pull of pride, we take on a sense of awe-inspiring accomplishment. One such experience goes as follows.

Nicole's marriage began with infinite optimism. At the matrimonial celebration the groom, 6'3" and 250 pounds of rippling muscle, stood at the altar as her knight in shining armor. The visible side of his personality was praised by his university, the public, and his friends. The college he attended voted Jake into their Athletic Hall of Fame as he excelled in track and field. Thus gifted, he was invited for tryouts on the US Olympic team. A man among men he was, with countless athletic accomplishments to prove it.

Nicole perceived Jake from a different perspective. Although his athleticism stood out, Nicole saw him through a lover's eyes. He was thoughtful, gentle, captivating and possessed the ability to indulge Nicole's interest in social justice, in which she would earn a PhD. For the first six years Jake lived up to his top billing in all departments, be it business, sports world, or a loving mate.

However, by the end of their seventh-year anniversary, Jake's invisible side became distressingly transparent. In the privacy of their home, behind very guarded closed doors, Jake commenced living out the aftereffects of an abusive childhood. Where friends relished his engaging personality, Nicole contended with the ugliness of Jake's mental wounds left by his abusive father.

The marriage partnership expanded to include women, alcohol, drugs, and limitless business nights away from home. Nicole's ominous secret was much too poisonous to be poured out into the community. Doing so would've been lethal to her and the children, so Nicole torturously labored to coat her sadness by smearing on counterfeit smiles at home and in public. In hiding Jake's fabrications, Nicole became a lie herself, transforming her into a spiritual, emotional, and physical wreck.

That which Nicole couldn't keep concealed from the children was Jake's absenteeism as a father. He rarely attended school functions, be it academic or sports related. When he did step up as a father, he was the critical parent, forever finding fault with his daughter's soccer ability or his son's lack of quickness playing peewee football. Any quality time he offered at their functions was directed to the more talented youngsters. His children mourned the death of a father's love while Nicole grieved over the ending of her marriage.

The nightmare escalates

During routine housework, Nicole was traumatized when discovering crack cocaine and bricks of marijuana hidden in wastebaskets and clothes hampers. When Nicole confronted Jake he pledged to repent, and he did, he altered where he hid his drugs. As Jake's chemical dependency grew, he became indifferent to Nicole's uncovering his secret life. When Nicole uncovered hardcore pornography magazines at the bottom of the children's toy box, she began to question her own performance as a wife. If she would've remained a newlywed in the bedroom, if she would've been more active in Jake's world of sports, if she would've been spit spot in the tidiness of their home, if she would've devoted more time to her physical attractiveness, if she would've placed her dream of achieving a doctorate degree on hold, if she would have enriched her skills in the kitchen, if she wasn't a stick in the mud when it came to weekly/nightly parties. If, if, if. The reason for attacking herself was obvious. The ifs were things she could've changed, therefore, there was hope. After months of applying those "ifs" in her everyday life to no avail, she exhaustedly raised the white flag.

Up until then, Nicole was adamant the family's personal business be kept under lock and key. Now, sitting in her vehicle, out of the children's hearing, she phoned a professional counselor. That evening, Nicole informed Jake of her decision to see a counselor while inviting him to join her. He declined the offer; however, he did the unexpected. First thing the following morning, before coffee, before hygiene protocol, Jake charged into the kitchen broadcasting, "Never in a million years". He couldn't be the person or husband she aspired him to be, "Never." With that, he nervously and hastily exited her presence while clumsily stumbling into the archway on his way out.

Nicole's aspiration and determination of holding off the guillotine to her marriage finally came slicing down, severing the final bit of hope she had hung unto for years.

As weeks turned into months, news of her household secrets whooshed through the neighborhood like a winter wind. Nicole attempted quieting the gossip gale through muteness as she was determined to live out God's word found in Titus 3:2, "to speak evil of no one, to be peaceable, gentle, showing all humility to all men."

Hold a grudge or have prayers answered

The day Nicole received legal papers asserting the divorce was final was the day reality set in. Sixteen years of marriage and motherhood, there she stood papers in hand, pronouncing her a single parent. Fuming thoughts of retaliation, those reprisals she vowed never to succumb to, stormed her conscience. An all-out spiritual war was readying. Darkness opposing light, evil challenging virtue as Nicole, at the moment, wanted nothing to do with God's word in Romans 12:19, "'Vengeance is Mine, I will repay,' says the Lord." Her reasoning was that she read the story of Jonah, and Jonah's fears were her own struggles. Jonah 4:1–2: "But it displeased Jonah exceedingly, and he became angry. So he prayed to the LORD, and said, 'Ah, LORD, was not this what I said when I was still in my country? Therefore, I fled previously to Tarshish; for I know that You are a gracious and merciful God, slow to anger and abundant in lovingkindness, One who relents from doing harm'." Nicole knew from her own life experiences God was merciful and granted second chances. Nevertheless, at the time, her temperament wasn't in favor of God exhibiting benevolence to Jake that she herself received time and again. Wearing a yoke of bitterness weighed her down as she began living out Romans 7:15: "For what I am doing, I do not understand. For what I will to do, that I do not practice; but what I hate, that I do."

Then, during one of her nightly prayers and reading God's word, she came face-to-face with her darkness. She read Romans 14:10: "Therefore let us pursue the things which make for peace and the things by which one may edify another." The only thing she was pursuing was hate. Then came 1 Corinthians 9:24–27: "Do you not know that those who run in a race all run, but one receives the prize? Run in such a way that you may obtain it. And everyone who competes for the prize is temperate in all things. Now they do it to obtain a perishable crown, but we for an imperishable crown. Therefore, I run thus: not with uncertainty. Thus, I fight: not as one who beats the air. But I discipline my body and bring it into subjection, lest, when I have preached to others, I myself should become disqualified." She was mentally in a race alright, and her opponent was revenge. Then came a ray of light bursting through her darkness. As she read Acts 1:8, "But you shall receive power when the Holy Spirit has come upon you; and you shall be witnesses to Me in Jerusalem, and in all Judea and Samaria, and to the end of the earth," tears of joy gushed down her face.

God's word proclaimed she possessed the power through the Holy Spirit, to defeat her battle with evil. When the question is asked: "Would Nicole succeed in overcoming a mind-set of darkness?" The answer was and is today, it will depend on Nicole's frame of mind. As time passed, she began living out Philippians 3:12–14: "Not that I have already attained, or am already perfected; but I press on, that I may lay hold of that for which Christ Jesus has also laid hold of me. Brethren, I do not count myself to have apprehended; but one thing I do, forgetting those things which are behind and reaching forward to those things which are ahead, I press toward the goal for the prize of the upward call of God in Christ Jesus." No longer did she expect God to do the supernatural by changing her heart while she slept. God, in the Spirit, was within her; she needed only to go forward while living out God's word. God would supply the strength for facing each new challenge she faced.

Turning to us, it's the Spirit of God within us that guarantees triumph over the forces of evil. We can turn the cheek every now and then, but Jesus isn't requesting us to be merciful once in a while or when there's little at stake. It's a lifestyle, and like Nicole, through prayer, plus putting into practice God's word, we too can navigate through those destructive minefields of hate and revenge

Mercy giving sets our conscious free

When showing mercy, there takes place a wonderful liberation. Months later, when Nicole was questioned on why she didn't attempt to cause her husband embarrassment, or destroy his reputation, she replied, that if she didn't hold on to Jesus's teachings of love which included forgiveness, she'd be making a mockery of God's forbearance in her own life. If she was to find her identity in Jesus, it would entail following Christ's lead as displayed by Jesus in Luke 23:39–43:

> Then one of the criminals who were hanged blasphemed Him, saying, "If You are the Christ, save Yourself and us." But the other, answering, rebuked him, saying, "Do you not even fear God, seeing you are under the same condemnation? And we indeed justly, for we receive the due reward of our deeds; but this Man has done nothing wrong." Then he said to Jesus, "Lord, remember me when You come into Your kingdom." And Jesus said to him, "Assuredly, I say to you, today you will be with Me in Paradise."

The above drama was scarcely minutes from Christ's physical ministry on earth coming to a close. His final work was to allocate grace to the thief in place of justice, forgiveness in place of getting what he deserves. The last thing the sinner should wish of God was to be fair at the time of judgment. Right is right and wrong is wrong, that's fair. A story will assist with understanding this thinking.

The late Reverend Dr. R. C. Sproul told of a time when he was teaching a college class where he illustrated through a factual experience that mercy forever wins out over justice.

The first day of class, R.C. assigned a written paper due back on his desk in two weeks. The day the project was to be completed, 40 percent of the class was not prepared.

Students, one after another, imparted rationale for their non-readiness. Subsequently, Dr. Sproul extended the due date for one week. The following week, 25 percent of the class was negligent. Students pleaded and pleaded for mercy, citing well-thought-out excuses before the professor allotted one final week.

The day arrived, and not to the professor's surprise, 15 percent had nothing to show for an extra three weeks of postponements. When students solicited for one more extension, the professor drew a line in the sand. From that 15 percent, there were students with the audacity to say, "Dr. Sproul, you're not fair."

With that, the professor picked up his grade book and began calling out names. "Smith, do you have your paper to turn in?"

No came the reply.

The professor barked out, "F. Jones, do you have your paper to be turned in."

No came the reply.

The professor again barked out, "F," while looking out at the class, "For four weeks I gave grace, kindness beyond what you deserved. Today, you demanded fairness, and fairness you received. Each and every one of the students who abused the time frame received an "F."

Looking at the thief's situation, he was without hope. There wasn't time left on his earthly clock to turn his life around. The beauty of this story is mercy is given to the thief, not justice. Jesus declared in Luke 23:43, "Today you will be with Me in Paradise."

Matthew 6:14–15 says, "For if you forgive men their trespasses, your heavenly Father will also forgive you. But if you do not forgive men their trespasses, neither will your Father forgive your trespasses." Consequently, to deny mercy giving when possessing the power to show benevolence, is to interrupt fellowship with God.

There's hope for those longing to be merciful!

First, for the believers to love their enemy requires a power outside themselves. Romans 8:26a says, "Likewise the Spirit also helps in our weaknesses." One weakness the believer struggles with is turning the cheek. Relying on our own strength to exhibit compassion resembles a failed New Year's resolution. It may work, and, then again, it may not. Living hope on the other hand is hope placed not in ourselves but in Jesus Christ. 1 Peter 1:3 says, "Blessed be the God and Father of our Lord Jesus Christ, who according to His abundant mercy has begotten us again to a living hope through the resurrection of Jesus Christ from the dead." "Living" hope offers high expectation to the believer. Scripture announces in 2 Chronicles 20:15, "for the battle is not yours, but God's." To triumph in exhibiting mercy lies in the power of the Holy Spirit.

Secondly, as a believer lives a life of mercygiving, a liberating experience takes place. To be set free from grudges and resentments that drain self-worth from one's character, is deeply gratifying. Which means mercy giving is deeply therapeutic.

In the gospel of Luke are instructions on how to break the chains of disobedience. Luke 6:38 says, "Give, and it will be given to you: good measure, pressed down, shaken together, and running over will be put into your bosom. For with the same measure that you use, it will be measured back to you." A good measure of mercy isn't skimpy. Nor is it something we begrudgingly hand out. Mercy extended will be a mercy received. It is promised by God in Psalm 23:6 which says, "Surely goodness and mercy shall follow me all the days of my life." And God's compassions never fail says Lamentations 3:22–23: "Through the Lord's mercies we are not consumed, because His compassions fail not. They are new every morning; great is Your faithfulness." God is an inexhaustible spring of leniency, desiring to open the flood gates that carry the believer into a higher experience of God's love.

Living mercifully instead of practicing hardheartedness confirms Christ's involvement in our lives. In Philippians 3:10, Paul writes, "that I may know Him and the power of His resurrection, and the fellowship of His sufferings, being conformed to His death." We become eyewitness to the power of His resurrection, when living life compassionately. Turning the cheek is nothing more than sharing in our Savior's sufferings. How good is that!? And the act of mercy giving reveals the spiritual health of our soul.

It's inspiring when we imitate Christ's mercy giving rather than wallowing in the mud of justice, rendering to a person who's hurt us, what they deserve. Ephesians 5:1 says, "Therefore be imitators of God as dear children." I'm first to confess, imitating Christ's mercy can appear beyond reach. Isaiah himself tasted hopelessness when he was overcome by the beauty of God in Isaiah 6:5. "He moaned, 'Woe is me! For I am undone; because I am a man of unclean lips and I live among a people of unclean lips'." Left to ourselves, without the mercy of Christ, we ourselves must proclaim, "Woe is me."

For those who ignore Christ's command to be merciful, Jesus's words are harsh. Matthew 23:23 says, "Woe to you, scribes and Pharisees, hypocrites! For you pay tithe of mint and anise and cummin, and have neglected the weightier matters of the law: justice and mercy and faith."

Exhibiting clemency is a very weighty matter, for it's God's second greatest commandment. To love one another, the way Christ loves us, is to live life compassionately. As trying as that may be, when that's accomplished, is to be living out God's commands. Deuteronomy 10:12 says, "He has shown you, O man, what is good; And what does the Lord require of you but to do justly, To love mercy, And to walk humbly with your God?"

So here is the sweetness that dilutes the tart. Blessed are the merciful, for they shall obtain mercy.

CHAPTER 7

Blessed Are the Pure in Heart,
for They Shall See God

—Matthew 5:8

In the preface, I commented on why Jesus was able to attract crowds. One form of motivation came from accounts of the extraordinary wonders Jesus brought about. For example, in Matthew 9:5–8, those who gathered were eyewitnesses to His marvels. "For which is easier, to say, 'Your sins are forgiven you,' or to say, 'Arise and walk'? But that you may know that the Son of Man has power on earth to forgive sins—then He said to the paralytic, 'Arise, take up your bed, and go to your house.' And he arose and departed to his house." Those in attendance must have mulled over the idea, "if Jesus brought to life paralytic legs, what might He do for them?"

Accordingly, when Christ promised blessings to those poor in Spirit, and to those who mourned, the crowd must have gone bonkers. The reason being they knew that on more than one occasion, they disobeyed God's commands. Which meant, if they mourned their secret sins, they were in for a miracle of their own. Christ's words of hope were music to their ears and oh how sweet the sound!

That is, until Jesus announces, "Blessed are the 'pure' in heart, for they shall see God." Jesus didn't say blessed are those who've practiced foot washings, or blessed are those who've refrained from work on the Sabbath. If He had mentioned such works, smiles would've broken out like an epidemic. But He didn't. It's the condition of the heart Jesus points to, the heart spoken of in Jeremiah17:9: "The heart is deceitful above all things, and desperately wicked; who can know it?" When Jesus unexpectedly declared, "Blessed are the 'pure' in Heart, for they will see God," the crowd's enthusiasm certainly diminished wondering to themselves, What constitutes a pure heart? Do I have one?

What Jesus meant was possessing a heart untainted. If Jesus was referring to a heart without blemish, there wasn't a person in the crowd, or anyplace else for that matter, who qualified. Nonetheless, in Psalm 24:1–5 are these words: "The earth is the LORD's, and all its fullness, the world and those who dwell therein. For He has founded it upon the seas, and established it upon the waters. Who may ascend into the hill of the LORD? Or who may stand in His holy place? He who has clean hands and a pure heart, who has not lifted up his soul to an idol, nor sworn deceitfully. He shall receive blessing from the LORD, and righteousness from the God of his salvation."

Jesus's cutting words provoked an uneasy consciousness not present when Jesus initially commenced speaking. Ephesians 6:6 says it this way, "not with eye service, as men-pleasers, but as bondservants of Christ, doing the will of God from the heart, with goodwill doing service, as to the Lord, and not to men."

When King David governed Israel, the people looked upon him as a man among men. However, as powerful as King David was, he was no match for overcoming his very human mind and heart. King David was well versed in how abruptly fleshly appetites can overrule good judgment. He cried out in Psalm 51:10, "Create in me a clean heart, O God, and renew a steadfast spirit within me." David isn't asking for success over his physical enemies to preserve his expansive reputation. He's petitioning to triumph where the battle is severest, in the inner self.

Why was David concerned with realizing internal triumph of the heart? 1 Samuel 16:7 offers insight. "For the LORD does not see as man sees; for man looks at the outward appearance, but the LORD looks at the heart." God's main objective for the believer isn't how many people we share Christ with. The focus of Jesus words is meant to penetrate beyond the intellect. Psalm 57:7 says, "My heart is steadfast, O God, my heart is steadfast." The passage implies that a heart for God is the first requirement in worship.

In the book of 2 Samuel, King David came face-to-face with the painful truth that his heart was double-minded. David uncomfortably experienced what scripture promises in Numbers 32:23, "but if you do not do so, then take note, you have sinned against the LORD; and be sure your sin will find you out." God sent David's servant, Nathan, with this message in 2 Samuel 23, "Why have you despised the commandment of the LORD, to do evil in His sight?" The great king, mighty in power, may have chastised Nathan, a mere servant, for having the audacity to challenge his personal decisions. However, upon hearing Nathan's soul-searching words, David groans, "I have sinned against the Lord." Nothing else needed to be said. David knelt before God, like previous times in the past crying out. "Have mercy upon me, O God, according to Your lovingkindness; According to the multitude of Your tender mercies, blot out my transgressions. Wash me thoroughly from my iniquity, and cleanse me from my sin" (Psalm 51:1–2). The love of God was the foundation in which David placed his hope for restoration from personal sin.

David's life, much like ours, had the teeter-totter effect. He desired honoring God but, was well acquainted with folly. Which means God's mercy through Jesus Christ is essential if we're to trek onward toward holiness.

So when Jesus said, "Blessed are the pure in heart," pure refers to not allowing rivals in regard to being dedicated to Emanuel. Matthew 6:21 warns, "For where your treasure is, there your heart will be also." Life becomes painful and messy when the heart answers to two masters.

Confession is good for heart problems

Purity of the heart involves confession. John 1:9 says, "If we confess our sins, he is faithful and just and will forgive us our sins and purify us from all unrighteousness."

The word "if" we confess our sins, implies that not all humble themselves before the Holy God. And without the self-effacement experience, purity is unattainable. With that said, to those who do humble themselves before God, confessing their sins, Jeremiah 34:4

offers magnificent words of hope. "I will forgive their iniquity and their sin I will remember no more."

Scripture is replete with statements acquiring a new heart. Ezekiel 11:19–20 say, "Then I will give them one heart, and I will put a new spirit within them, and take the stony heart out of their flesh, and give them a heart of flesh, that they may walk in My statutes and keep My judgments and do them; and they shall be My people, and I will be their God." Again, in Jeremiah 24:7, "Then I will give them a heart to know Me, that I am the Lord; and they shall be My people, and I will be their God, for they shall return to Me with their whole heart." A new heart is a heart for God that has no equals, no worldly gods to contend for the throne of glory. Deuteronomy 30:6 says, "And the Lord your God will circumcise your heart and the heart of your descendants, to love the Lord your God with all your heart and with all your soul, that you may live."

Making of a new heart

When we embrace Christ, our polluted heart is bathed in the purity of the Savior. In the Old Testament, in the book of 2 Kings, God ordered Naaman, a leper, to bathe in the Jordan for healing. At first, Naaman rejected such nonsense. However, as time went on, he submitted and experienced the miracle of divine cleansing. Ezekiel 37:14 says, "I will put My Spirit in you, and you shall live." The words, "And you shall live," indicate a higher ethical and spiritual life than previously possessed.

Secondly, "to live" means no longer under the reign of Satan. Hebrews 8:12 says, "For I will be merciful to their unrighteousness, and their sins and their lawless deeds I will remember no more." A pure heart is free to obey the commands of God, no longer obligated to follow the commands of Satan. A heart for God brings hope in all circumstances, be it joyful or heart-wrenching. The following are stories of people who when encountering God wanted more of His holiness.

Moses

During a routine workday overseeing his father-in-law's sheep, Moses was taken back when coming upon a brush fire. It's well documented lightning causes brush fires in regions with a deficiency of rain. However, common as brush fires may be, the one Moses came upon was distinct in that the shrub wasn't consumed by the blaze. The blaze resembled a gas burning fire place where the artificial logs remain unscathed.

The spectacle triggered Moses's curiosity to investigate and in doing so he heard his name being called out, "Moses, Moses."

Startled, Moses responded with nothing more than, "Here I am."

Immediately a second announcement followed. "Take your sandals off your feet, for the place where you stand is holy ground." The voice revealed the person behind the command: "I am the God of your father—the God of Abraham, the God of Isaac, and the God of Jacob. And Moses hid his face, for he was afraid to look upon God" (Exodus 3:5–6). That was to be the beginning of a friendship that grew into intimacy.

God directed Moses to the frontline in freeing Israel from Egypt and in doing so he witnessed firsthand the amazement of God. Pharaoh relished having captive Israel as free labor and had no intention of relinquishing his economic windfall. To pry Pharaoh's hands from his hold on Israel, God activated plague after plague upon the land. The outbreak weakened Pharaoh's resistance; however, when Pharaoh contemplated losing his unconventional workforce, the extremist measures by God became mandatory.

The Passover experience describes God's maximum determination. Exodus 11:4–6: "Thus says the LORD: 'About midnight I will go out into the midst of Egypt; and all the firstborn in the land of Egypt shall die, from the firstborn of Pharaoh who sits on his throne, even to the firstborn of the female servant who is behind the handmill, and all the firstborn of the animals. Then there shall be a great cry throughout all the land of Egypt, such as was not like it before, nor shall be like it again'."

Pharaoh's resistance at long last collapsed, permitting Israel to flee. Conversely, when the stench of death faded and the thought of the loss of Egypt's workforce, Pharaoh had a change of heart. Exodus 14:5: "The heart of Pharaoh and his servants was turned against the people; and they said, 'Why have we done this, that we have let Israel go from serving us?'" As cream comes to the top, so did money in Pharaoh's thinking. So he made ready his chariot and took his people with him.

Israel's march to freedom led them to the shores of the Red Sea. With the sea blocking Israel's advancement and the enemy closing from the rear, God ordered Moses to stretch out his hand over the sea. Exodus 14:21–23 says, "the LORD caused the sea to go back by a strong east wind all that night, and made the sea into dry land, and the waters were divided. So the children of Israel went into the midst of the sea on the dry ground, and the waters were a wall to them on their right hand and on their left." Once safely on the opposite bank, God again commands Moses, "Stretch out your hand over the sea that the waters may come back upon the Egyptians, on their chariots, and on their horsemen" It goes without saying, the pursuit of Pharaoh's army quickly died.

Moses, experiencing God in such a pronounced form, should have been sufficient for the remainder of his life. However, in Exodus 33:18, we hear Moses begging for more. "Please, show me Your glory." The Old Testament patriarch developed a thirst for the divine that was unquenchable.

David

Next, King David savored seeing God. Psalm 42:1–2 says, "As the deer pants for the water brooks, so pants my soul for You, O God. My soul thirsts for God, for the living God. When shall I come and appear before God?" David's aspiration for seeing God wasn't in hopes of being showered with material blessings. For David, God was the blessing.

To David, seeing God in all circumstances, good or bad, generated hope. When conditions of his life called for panic, David sought comfort from above. He lived believing Psalm 31:15, "My times are in God's hands." For David, all the varied events in life were under God's guidance. In Psalm 23:3, David shouts, "He leadeth me in the paths of righteousness." David was acutely aware of God's total involvement in his life.

As heart and mind become undivided in loyalty to God, scripture points to the following taking place, "they shall see God" (Matthew 5:8). To see God is first to see ourselves as we actually are. Isaiah said in Isaiah 6:6, "Woe is me, for I am undone! Because I am a man of unclean lips, and I dwell in the midst of people of unclean lips; for my eyes had seen the King, the Lord of hosts." Discovering the truth about ourselves comes by the power and love of God, which gives evidence we're being remolded by the potter of the universe.

In the gospel of St Luke 5:8, when Peter came face-to-face with Christ's power and glory, "he fell at Jesus' knees and said, go away from me, for I'm a sinful man." In conclusion, when Paul, God's right-hand man, beheld God's beauty, he cried out, "This is a faithful saying and worthy of all acceptance, that Christ Jesus came into the world to save sinners of whom I am chief" (1 Timothy 1:15).

Without God's assistance, the four, Isaiah, Job, Peter, and Paul, would've become sinful prideful servants, for their lives were chockfull of God sightings to boast about. Yet, as they compared God's beauty alongside their foulness, they cried out for mercy. The brilliance not only for David, but for you and me, when grasping the certainty of our sinfulness, God is awakening us and thus preparing us for genuine worship.

In the narrative that follows, Marcus, similar to Isaiah, Job, Peter, and Paul, grasped a new perspective of Jesus. In doing so, he was made aware of his spiritual shortcomings, and as a result, purity of heart for him became a real possibility.

Marcus, a homeowner, was experiencing plumbing problems. Off and on for over a year, his lavatory and shower stopped up, creating a huge mess. The toilet plunger was on duty around the clock. Marcus pointed his finger to the children, believing they were the culprits for using too much paper. However, as time went on, even with the children being watchful, the problem worsened.

A plumber brought in a camera to run through the sewer line. One pass and the problem was discovered. Not solved, mind you, but detected. Marcus's sewer pipe traveled underground, across the street, attaching to the city's main sewer line. Six feet from the city's main, Marcus's sewer pipe was broken. Which explained why paper and stuff clogged the flow. What wasn't so easy to explain was how a pipe, buried six feet in the ground, was crushed. In time, that mystery would be uncovered. The difficulty at the moment was getting to the broken pipe required tedious excavating. Beneath the ground where digging was to take place were hundreds of telephone wires leading to homes throughout the community. With shovels in hand, five high school boys burrowed down like ground hogs, and before sunset, the problem was solved. And to add to Marcus's joy, the workers uncovered the reason for the pipe breakage. A year earlier in burying fiber optics, a phone company's trencher cut through the pipe. Marcus's children were inside celebrating, pointing their finger at Dad saying, "We told you we didn't cause the problem." With the blockage problem solved and the phone company taking full responsibility, Marcus's nightmare was behind him, or so he thought.

The correct procedure for settling up with the plumbing company was for Marcus to pay the plumbing company the price agreed upon. He would then send the receipt to the fiber optics company for reimbursement. However, the following day, when Marcus arrived at the office of the plumbing company to settle up, he was met with another surprise. The plumbing company offered to invoice the phone company rather than Marcus. Marcus returned home, but not for the better.

The part wiping the smile off Marcus's countenance came when the phone company baulked paying the plumbing business their unreasonable price. The invoice was four times the amount quoted by Marcus. Too large of a business to be bullied, the phone company denied payment. Six months later, the plumbing business, knowing they wouldn't win their fight with Goliath, accepted what was offered. Nevertheless, greed by the plumbing company set out to take on the smaller in stature, and Marcus was summoned to small claims court and lost. A handshake agreeing doesn't mean much now days, in or out of court.

For months, Marcus's old sinful nature, passionate for revenge, thought up ways to even the score. The test revealed Marcus's old sinful nature remained extremely energetic. Passing of time did little to heal wounded pride, until he read Isaiah 53:7. "He was oppressed and He was afflicted, Yet He opened not His mouth; He was led as a lamb to the slaughter, and as a sheep before its shearers is silent, So He opened not His mouth," Marcus read, wept, and ultimately grasped Christ's silence was for him. It appeared to Marcus that the world had turned on him and that vengeance was his only recourse, nonetheless, in doing so, Marcus would have turned on Jesus. Marcus felt Job's, Peter's, and Paul's emotions when they consciously encountered God. Not through imagining or envisioning but through the awakening of his soul to the exquisiteness of Christ's presence.

Sanctification, transformation

1 Thessalonians 4:3 offers one last insight. "For this is the will of God, your sanctification." The word transformation aids in conveying the meaning of the word sanctification. This transformation (sanctification) is a lifelong process where the Holy Spirit composes in us a prize to be presented to God.

If you're like me, when we sin, we question if spiritual transformation ever was an ongoing process. Yet, in times of wonderment, scripture offers hope. 2 Peter 3:9 says, "The Lord is not slack concerning His promise, as some count slackness, but is longsuffering toward us, not willing that any should perish but that all should come to repentance." God's promising miracle work on our very damaged hearts imparts hope for the grand day ahead.

In closing, I return to Ezekiel 11:19: "I will give them one heart, and I will put a new spirit within them, and take the stony heart out of their flesh, and give them a heart of flesh." Blessed are the pure in heart and blessed are those that a pure heart is in the making. Philippians 1:6 says, "Being confident of this very thing, that He who began a good work in you will perfect it until the day of Jesus Christ."

Chapter 8

Blessed Are the Peacemakers, for They Shall
be Called the Children of God

—Matthew 5:9

This past week my cell phone rang, and the caller, Sara, who I knew from her being a member of one of my past congregations, wasn't her normal bubbly self. Following a few hurried words of greetings, Sara shared her agony. Her first cousin's daughter, age early twenties, was murdered. Painfully, Sara attempted to explain why she phoned.

Three years ago her cousin Martha, and husband Richard, moved out of state due to Richard being transferred. Martha never protested being forced to part from family and friends; nevertheless, her heart silently and continually grieved the loss of kinfolk's support. When her daughter, Megan, was slain, Martha declared her daughter's body would go back to the sacred burial grounds with the nearest and dearest. Without offering any more information, Sara inquired if I would officiate the funeral. Agreeing that I would, Sara would relay the information to the grieving parents, who would be in contact.

The following day, the traumatized father phoned, desperate to safely release bottled up fury. With the deceased daughter's children staying at his home, the unspoken rule was, visibly grieving was to be kept to a minimum. Consequently, when the grandchildren inquired on when would Mommy be undead, hate for the assassin consumed Richard, and he needed desperately to discharge his resentment.

We met in the church sanctuary where Megan's memorial service was to be held the following morning. Martha and Richard seated themselves in the front pew of the church and, for two hours, agonizingly recounted their nightmare.

It all began a year past, when their daughter phoned asking if she and her two young daughters could move in for a time. Hence, within days of receiving her parents' blessing, Megan and her children packed up what belongings they possessed, hopeful of a new beginning.

Within forty-five days of her moving to Michigan, Megan found employment and shortly after that, she and the children moved into their own apartment. As weeks turned into months, Megan launched into a relationship soon to be a live-in. Almost immediately Megan faced the consequence of inadequate judgment. Unbeknownst to Megan, the live-in carried the herpes virus and, in short order, transmitted the disease to Megan. With no cure for the infection, Megan deemed herself trapped. Agonized over being infected with a sexually transmitted disease, she mentally scuffled over how to terminate the relationship. Dreadful of his reaction, she made the irrational decision to remain silent and do nothing. That is, until large outbreaks on her vagina emerged.

Megan dropped off the radar one Wednesday evening. Routinely, she phoned her parents before picking up the children after work. On this date, evening came and with that darkness until the clock struck 11:00 p.m. No Megan. On what seemed like the hundredth time looking at the kitchen clock, Martha blurted out, "Megan, if you don't call by 11:30 p.m., I'm punching in the numbers 9-1-1." At exactly 11:31 p.m., she phoned the police.

Within hours, the police, Martha, Richard and the landlord entered Megan's apartment. Nothing appeared out of the ordinary. Dirty dishes in the kitchen sink, a wastebasket needing emptied, a man's shirt draped over a chair and unopened mail on the living room table.

Things seemed normal until opening the door to the bathroom. The cold water to the basin was running and, on the floor, a white bunched up bath mat with spotted stains.

Moving on down the hall, the children's bedroom was next. Opening the door, a Winnie the Pooh lighted lamp revealed nothing out of the ordinary. Along with a baby doll sleeping in her crib were toys in, around, and under the girls' beds. The setting told of well-being, and besides, the children were safe and sound at Grandma's home.

Martha paused and then pointed to the master bedroom at the far end of the hall, and in so doing, the officer took the lead. Opening the door, and unlike the children's bedroom, the room was completely dark. The officer extended his arm around the door jam, feeling for the toggle switch. Instantly, the light uncovered a horror Martha and Richard were protected from witnessing. At once, the officer flipped the switch off, closed the door, and gently resolved to guide Martha and Richard back through the apartment and outside.

The police report told of Megan lying face down on the floor. Her once straw-colored hair now appeared as a soaked rag mop laying in a pool of blood. Without going into further details, the crime scene told of evil and, with a bloodied knife and scissors lying close to Megan's body, communicated just how evil.

On Tuesday, the day before finding Megan's body, her live-in was pulled from Megan's inflamed automobile. At the hospital, he told police he was smoking pot and must have fallen asleep. Richard and Martha were left to speculate that their daughter informed her live-in he had to leave. Accosted by rejection, he retaliated with acts of malicious savagery and then attempted to commit suicide.

At the conclusion of Martha and Richard's grueling story, a welcomed calm fell over the sanctuary. For the longest time, the three of us sat in silence, reluctant to disturb the calm. Minutes pass before I softly inquired, "Angry at God?"

Martha, staring at the floor faintly murmured, "No."

Turning my eyes toward Richard, his head slowly nodded in the affirmative. For him, God watched as evil was given permission to destroy his daughter. In questioning God's benevolence, Richard's restrained anger broke loose. Peacemakers stay close to the hurting while not interfering with the healing process. I break from the story to put a spotlight on what isn't peacemaking.

Supposedly a "peace-making team," made up of a group of men from a local church visited their congregation's shut-ins. One such visit was to the home of a man who had severe Parkinson's disease. Crippled physically, having little control of voluntary muscles, he welcomed the church's visit. As the visit came to a close, one member of the peace-making team made this comment, "if you had more faith Tom, you'd get up out of that chair and start walking." That's not peacemaking in the strongest sense of the word. Housed in a peacemaker's heart is compassion, not religious arrogance. Now, back to Martha and Richard.

In silence, I pondered what next to say or do. Do I quote scripture, such as Romans 8: 28: "And we know that all things work together for good to those who love God, to those who are the called according to His purpose." Absolutely not. Romans 12:15 gives perfect directions in this circumstance. "Rejoice with those who rejoice, and weep with those who weep." The result of being a genuine peacemaker, the hurting can safely share doubts of God's love, involvement, and existence, without being judged or chastised.

Once Martha and Richard revisited their traumatic reality and became quiet following emptying themselves of bottled up anger, I was hesitant to ask them to join me in prayer. However, when I did, Richard was first to bow his head in a beautiful act of submission. It wasn't his heart questioning the character or existence of God, rather a frayed and traumatized mind. And peacemakers recognize the difference. Richard needed a peacemaker, someone tangible to assist him in seeing God, the intangible. You, the reader, are called to be God's peacemakers.

The day of the memorial service, the sanctuary was filled with friends and family eager to share commemorations of Megan. Tribute followed tribute as friends came forward with joyful memories. Peacemaking was well on its way as I approached the microphone to give the eulogy.

I commenced by saying, "We're reminded in the Bible, God's children often suffer terribly." I then read a passage from 2 Corinthians 1:8: "For we do not want you to be ignorant, brethren, of our trouble which came to us in Asia: that we were burdened beyond measure, above strength, so that we despaired even of life." I looked out at those attending the memorial and said, "Who would understand the meaning of the word burdened better than Megan's children, or her mom, and dad? Their burden is so excessively huge it cannot be measured. In times like these, Satan quickly moves beside the bereaved, not to encourage but to fill the troubled soul with doubts of the whereabouts of a loving God." It's here that God's peacemakers warmly pass hope to the hopeless.

In the message, I told of Job in the Old Testament who went through similar sufferings of losing family. It began when Job received news the enemy raided his land and fled with all the oxen and donkeys. Moments later, a second messenger appears, declaring fire of God fell from heaven and burned up all Job's sheep and with the third messenger informing Job of a raiding party stealing Job's camels, his life savings vanished, sealing financial collapse. Those quick to place a religious twist to the circumstances would hint, "Chin up, you still have family and health." That is until the final messenger arrives declaring, "Job, your children are all dead."

Job's youngsters had gotten together at the oldest son's house when an eruption from a storm struck the house and all were trapped inside. Job's wife mentally cracked, lashing out at Job saying, "Do you still hold fast to your integrity? Curse God and die!" Her frustrated outcry gave evidence of Satan's involvement. At first, it doesn't sound as if Job is a peacemaker with his strong response to his wife's outburst in Job 2:10 "Shall we indeed accept good from God, and shall we not accept adversity? In all this Job did not sin with his lips." Job's wife needed support with the uncertainties regarding God's involvement in man's pain. Job doesn't foolishly attempt to illuminate the mysteries of the deity. He simply points to the past and reminds his wife something on the lines of what Jonny Lange wrote about in the song entitled, "Who Made the Mountain."

> Who made the mountains, who made the trees
> Who made the rivers flow to the sea
> And who sends the rain when the earth is dry
> Somebody bigger than you and I

> When we're filled with despair
> Who gives me courage to go from there
> And who gives me faith that will never die
> Somebody bigger than you and I.

Next, I turned to the cry of Jesus from the cross in Mark 15:34: "My God, My God, why have You forsaken Me?" Christ's outcry didn't mean He ceased trusting God any more than Job's wife's sudden reaction to her children's death meant she didn't believe. Grieving plays a large part in God's plan for our lives.

Abraham of the Old Testament comes to mind when pondering the part suffering plays toward closeness with the Creator. In Genesis 22:2, we find Abraham in agony after God calls to him. "Abraham!" And he said, "Here I am." Then He said, "Take now your son, your only son Isaac, whom you love, and go to the land of Moriah, and offer him there as a burnt offering on one of the mountains of which I shall tell you." Abraham conceals his anguish from his son, Isaac. In verse 7, Isaac questions his father on the whereabouts of the lamb for the burnt offering? Isaac, well versed on sacrifices, knew something didn't add up. Abraham answered Isaac by saying, "My son, God will provide for Himself the lamb for a burnt offering." Abraham reassures his son that God is in control. Peacemakers are people who have absorbed, through life experiences of both pain and rejoicing, God isn't dead.

Galatians 2:20 says, "I have been crucified with Christ; it is no longer I who live, but Christ lives in me; and the life which I now live in the flesh I live by faith in the Son of God, who loved me and gave Himself for me." It goes without saying, blessed indeed is the person who embraces God's peace. To experience such calm comes by way of Christ having absolute say in one's decision making. I dare say, Paul's analysis of himself in Romans 7 comes close to where we are in the struggle to live Christlike lives. Roman 7:6 says, "For what I am doing, I do not understand. For what I will to do, that I do not practice; but what I hate, that I do."

Life can be described as an endless war of choosing. On the one hand, there's the urgings of goodness, while on the other is the pull to wander from the safeguards of graciousness. Part of us is a snake, and the other a butterfly. For the most part, we're not sure which will carry the day as choosing light over darkness is a continuous exercise. This means a peacemaker must be a person of prayer and self-examination.

In the book of John, chapter 14, verse 27, it says, "Peace I leave with you; my peace I give to you; not as the world gives do I give to you." What could be more sought after than a life absent of mental torment brought about by fearful imagination? Paul writes in Philippians 4:6–7, "Be anxious for nothing, but in everything by prayer and supplication, with thanksgiving, let your requests be made known to God; and the peace of God, which surpasses all understanding, will guard your hearts and minds through Christ Jesus."

Richard and Martha will never understand, on this side of heaven, why all things, including the slaying of their daughter, work for good to them whom Jesus is their savior. Nonetheless, peacemakers are encouraged to hold fast to sharing the message of hope in Christ to the hurting. The reward for your labor is in Isaiah 52:7 "How beautiful upon the mountains are the feet of him who brings good news, who proclaims peace, who brings glad tidings of good things, who proclaims salvation, who says to Zion, Your God reigns!"

Peacemakers shall be called the sons of God

To come to an understanding that the living God has a heart for the downcast raises our hopes as we go forward. Deuteronomy 32:10 says, "He found him in a desert land and in the wasteland, a howling wilderness; He encircled him, He instructed him, He kept him as the apple of His eye."

This passage points to experiencing a wilderness encounter. God took great pains with a sinful people by nurturing, educating, and leading them into His holy presence. At the time, Israel wasn't hungering for a life of righteousness. Nonetheless, God brought them into His protection. That care is ours when we accept Christ as our Savior and our treasure. Blessed are the peacemakers.

CHAPTER 9

Blessed Are Those Who Are Persecuted
for Righteousness Sake

—Matthew 5:10

In the book of Daniel, the story of Shadrach, Meshach, and Abed-Nego is a brilliant case study on how to glorify God when persecuted. The story unfolds with some jealous busybodies, (they're in every church) stirring up trouble. Like the snake that tempted Eve in the garden, these human serpents were hissing in the king's ear. Their complaint was over the three Jewish lads not following the king's decree. It's not surprising to find these Jewish lads, who paid homage to the living God, hassled. For they outwardly projected their beliefs for all to see, as Paul states in 2 Timothy 1:12, "I am not ashamed, of the Gospel."

Yet, in today's world, many attending Sunday worship would have little difficulty joining in on the king's decree. Never mind the narrow way Jesus spoke about in Matthew 7:13–14, "Enter by the narrow gate; for wide is the gate and broad is the way that leads to destruction, and there are many who go in by it. Because narrow is the gate and difficult is the way which leads to life, and there are few who find it."

In times when our faith is in question, Jesus clearly explains what's required. Matthew 16:24 says, "If anyone desires to come after Me, let him deny himself, and take up his cross, and follow Me." So when King Nebuchadnezzar pressured Shadrach, Meshach, and Abed-Nego, by saying in Daniel 3:14, "Is it true, Shadrach, Meshach, and Abed-Nego, that you do not serve my gods or worship the gold image which I have set up?" If not committed to their convictions, they, without doubt, would have chosen the wider way. It's the way of least resistance, not to mention avoiding a fiery furnace.

Nevertheless, how encouraging for those taking God's word seriously, to read of others who have chosen the narrow way. The three Jewish lads chose to burn, rather than turn. In Daniel 3:16–17, we read of their courage. "Nebuchadnezzar, we have no need to answer you in this matter. If that is the case, our God whom we serve is able to deliver us from the burning fiery furnace, and he will deliver us from your hand O king. But if not, let it be known to you, O king that we do not serve your gods."

Being deeply committed to worshipping the living God, the Jewish lads had no second thoughts. God held precedence, first and foremost, over any suffering they might encounter. For the believer today, 2 Timothy 3:12 adds to the support of Daniel by stating, "Yes, and all who desire to live godly in Christ Jesus will suffer persecution." So if you're committed to living for Christ, reckon on being the dart board rather than the dart.

For many years I struggled understanding Philippians 3:10, where it says, "that I may know Him and the power of His resurrection, and share in His sufferings, being conformed to His death." The struggle was over what sharing in Christ's sufferings looked like. Is it to suffer as Stephen did in Acts 7:59, "They stoned Stephen as he was calling on God." Or Paul's experience in 2 Corinthians 11:25: "I was beaten with rods; once I was stoned." If not by rocks or clubs, what does persecution to believers look like?

Merely experiencing difficulty isn't the persecution Jesus speaks of. For example, while traveling on a holiday weekend pulling a camper down Interstate 75, the transmission, without warning, quit. As our car lost power and speed, drivers behind us became impatient and exhibited their displeasure in assorted ways. That wasn't persecution.

Managing to maneuver the car out from among five lanes of traffic speeding seventy miles an hour plus to the side of the road wasn't persecution. Nor was it persecution when AAA sent two wreckers, one for the car, one for the trailer, and caravanned us into the parking lot of a truck dealership (although it felt like it).

When you live life based on 2 Corinthians 5:9, "making it your aim to be well pleasing to God," and you're singled out as a religious something, that's persecution of which Jesus speaks. In my childhood days, there was a saying, "I double dare you." The double dare was the greater challenge. The secular world today has double dared the Christian community saying, "Try living out your religious beliefs and see what happens." There's a price to be paid for speaking out regarding Christ teachings. Richard Dawkins, a leading atheist, encourages verbal bullying of those professing to be Christians. John 15:19 says, "If you were of the world, the world would love its own. Yet because you are not of the world, but I chose you out of the world, therefore the world hates you." So to avoid persecution today, one must remain silent, and to remain silent is to join Judas in the betrayal of Jesus.

Nevertheless, Christians can handle harassment when the mind-set is focused on pleasing God. 1 Peter 4:1 says, "Therefore, since Christ suffered for us in the flesh, arm yourselves also with the same mind, for he who has suffered in the flesh has ceased from sin." In the book of Chronicles, there's a war brewing in Jehoshaphat's life, but he's encouraged to fear not. 2 Chronicles 20:15 says, "Do not be afraid nor dismayed because of this great multitude, for the battle is not yours, but God's."

Turn your eyes on Jesus

The song, "Turn Your Eyes Upon Jesus," composed by Helen H. Lemmel was inspired through the writings of Lilias Trotter, in the early 1900s. After struggling in prayer for two years, Trotter came to the conclusion she must lay down her love of art in order to fix her eyes on Jesus, from which came, "Turn Your Eyes Upon Jesus."

> Turn your eyes upon Jesus
> Look full in His wonderful face
> and the things of earth will grow strangely dim
> in the light of His glory and grace.

SHOWERS OF BLESSINGS

Returning to Shadrach, Meshach, and Abed-Nego, the Jewish triad made a stand to honor their living God by not bowing down to the golden image. As a result, they were found guilty by the furious king over the lads' defiance and ordered executed by the most torturous way possible, burned alive. To the king's astonishment, he exclaims during the execution, "'Look!' he answered, 'I see four men loose, walking in the midst of the fire; and they are not hurt, and the form of the fourth is like the Son of God'"(Daniel 3:25).

The Jewish boys were spiritually strengthened time and again, witnessing for the greatness of God. While living out what they believed God was honored and in so doing, they were blessed. Not simply blessed by having their lives spared, which was no small thing, but blessed in their awareness of God. They were so aware of the presence of their Creator, God became practically tangible.

In this segment, I wish to pay tribute to my friend, Lorenzo, who I spoke of in chapter 3. He died during the writing of this book.

Through the encouragement of the Holy Spirit, from the moment Lorenzo parted ways with the penal institution, he strived to live life commendable to God. Galatians 6:2 was his go-to verse. "Bear one another's burdens, and so fulfill the law of Christ." There was a deep yearning to somehow, some way, make amends for the years of disrespect he had exhibited to one and all. That opportunity presented itself through blindly answering a help wanted ad. He was to appear for the interview in person. Upon entering a waiting room, an office girl greeted him with a large smile before speaking. "Mr. Pryor, I presume."

Lorenzo nodded followed by saying yes. He'd been called many names, but addressed as "Mr. Pryor" was foreign to his ears and a bit awkward. He wasn't in the waiting area long when the lady with the smile returned, inviting Lorenzo to follow her.

Lorenzo was conscious of the felony that most certainly would have a voice in this business meeting. Painfully aware of background checks, Lorenzo nervously spoke up. "Mr. Watkins, before you begin, if my getting hired is founded solely on the background check, it'll be a waste of your time to continue."

Mr. Watkins inquired, "How so?"

Lorenzo scuffled while uncrossing his legs, attempting to gather himself. At previous interviews, when given the opportunity to speak, he attempted to conceal his dark days of yesteryears. However, on this day, Lorenzo volunteered the crimes that took away his freedom. He finished by saying he was determined to live the rest of his life in a way his children and grandchildren would be proud of him.

Mr. Watkins leaned back in his office chair and said, "I'll look into your background before we meet again Mr. Pryor, but for now, please know I believe in second chances."

The following week, Lorenzo was officially employed as a forty-hour week full-time driver of a medical van ushering people to and from medical appointments. He was blessed, and God's mercy was revealing its self in every aspect of his personality.

My final phone conversation with Lorenzo was on a Friday evening. In that heart-seizing conversation, he directed the topic to his health. Until then, his focus was on his job. Only through the benefit of hindsight did I discover he was weighted down with a prognosis of cancer. Although mindful of the how sick he was, Lorenzo requested all further medical appointments not be during his working hours. He was contributing to the good of society which was commendable to God, and Lorenzo loved it. The autopsy report said he died Sunday night in bed.

Up until his death, he remained faithful to Christ. Rather than return to the street's he knew so well, he pressed on to lead a life pleasing to God. 2 Corinthians 4:9–10 says, "We are hard-pressed on every side, yet not crushed; we are perplexed, but not in despair; persecuted, but not forsaken; struck down, but not destroyed—always carrying about in the body the dying of the Lord Jesus, that the life of Jesus also may be manifested in our body."

I am honored to have known Lorenzo and grateful to God for bringing him into my life. Galatians 2:20: "I have been crucified with Christ; it is no longer I who live, but Christ lives in me; and the life which I now live in the flesh I live by faith in the Son of God, who loved me and gave Himself for me."

Chapter 10

In a Nutshell

I close by summarizing Jesus's "blessed are you" declarations. The crowd quieted when Jesus opened His mouth and taught them, saying, "blessed are the poor in spirit, for theirs is the kingdom of heaven." His message is a map that navigates us to the treasure we're in quest of—happiness. There is no mystery or riddle to consider, no hoops to jump through in attaining this long sought-after bliss. It's pure and simple, abandon self and cling to the mercy of Jesus as did the publican in Luke 18:13. "But the publican, standing afar off, would not lift up so much as his eyes unto heaven, but smote his breast, saying, God, be thou merciful to me a sinner." The publican didn't stand before God stating all his good deeds, rather like Psalm 131:2 states, "Like a weaned child is my soul within me." Poor in spirit is the person who embraces Jesus as the solitary way for fulfillment and salvation. The starting point in being blessed by God is admitting to ourselves we're spiritually destitute without the divine favor of Jesus Christ.

Blessed are those who mourn

When Jesus said, "Blessed are those who mourn," He wasn't directing our attention to all the heartaches we've suffered throughout life. The mourning Jesus speaks of is due to sins that leave us spiritually penniless. Matthew 11:28 says, "Come to me, all who are weary and heavy laden, and I will give you rest." Heavy laden is to drag around past and present wrongdoings against the holy God. The prodigal son understood mourning over a wayward life. Luke 15:18 says, "I will arise and go to my father, and will say to him, 'Father, I have sinned against heaven and before you, and I am no longer worthy to be called your son'." That's exactly what's required when we confess our sin against God. The result of such openness is found in Psalm 32:5: "And You forgave the iniquity of my sin."

Blessed are the meek

It's worth repeating, meekness is not weakness. A meek person has courage to come against the pride that often turns into a vengeful personality. Out of a truly meek personality can come a Christlike personality. In Hebrews 10:34, it says, "For you had compassion on me in my chains, and joyfully accepted the plundering of your goods, knowing that you have a better and an enduring possession for yourselves in heaven." In place of viewing life through a closed perspective, the meek take into consideration other's circumstances. The attention of the meek person isn't focused on themselves, but on what God desires of them. The psalmist says in 37:11, the result of humble living is, "They shall delight themselves in the abundance of peace."

Blessed are those who hunger and thirst for righteousness.

Those disconnected from worshipping God and those connected are on equal footing when it comes to hungering for happiness. The difference is how the two parties go about realizing fulfillment. Isaiah 55:2 puts it this way: "Why do you spend money for what is not bread, and your wages for what does not satisfy?" Exerting energy and time on things offering no eternal value is what Jeremiah terms broken cisterns. Jeremiah 2:13 says, "For My people have committed two evils: They have forsaken Me, the fountain of living waters, and hewn themselves cisterns—broken cisterns that can hold no water." To pursue happiness through material goods, achievements of all sorts, or recognition, we're promised a life similar to a broken cistern. Why labor for something that'll never bring about fulfillment when fulfillment is what you're seeking?

Blessed are the merciful

When Jesus spoke on being merciful, His focus was on the inner attitude. The good in the heart must become external to those around us. The merciful are to take on a visible attitude, responding to the hurting that Psalm 28:6 speaks of: "Blessed be the Lord, for he has heard the voice of my pleas for mercy." The merciful live life shackle free of resentment, judgment and unforgiveness while busying themselves uplifting the spirits of the down trodden.

Blessed are the pure in heart

When Jesus declares, blessed are the pure in heart, he's pointing to those who've been forgiven seventy times seven or unlimited times. Proverbs 2:9 says, "Who can say, "I have made my heart clean, I am pure from my sin?'" The question demands an answer and the response is no one except Jesus Christ. A mystifying exchange takes place when Jesus becomes the sinner's savior. Christ assigns His righteousness into the sinner's soul while simultaneously taking ownership of our indebtedness to God. At that moment, the believer becomes righteous, not in the sense of being righteous in character and conduct but rather in a blameless standing before God through Jesus Christ. The instant that mind-boggling trade takes place, there is peace with God, and our heart problem is resolved.

Blessed are those who are persecuted

Without a doubt, the eighth beatitude is my Achilles heel. Reading Jesus words, "Blessed are those who are persecuted," is where, for me, the spiritual bar is at its highest. I'm not keen on persecution, so when controversial subjects are debated, I've kept my opinion to myself. Nevertheless, the persecution Jesus addresses is rooted in religion. Luke 9:23 says, "If anyone desires to come after Me, let him deny himself, and take up his cross daily, and follow Me." To deny ourselves is to say once and for all, no to our old self of intimidation. Mark 8:3 says, "For whoever is ashamed of me and my words in this adulterous and sinful generation, of him also shall the Son of man be ashamed when he comes in the glory of his Father with his holy angels." Risking persecution for what is promised in Matthew 25:21: "Well done, good and faithful servant; you were faithful over a few things, I will make you ruler over many things. Enter into the joy of your Lord." It is worth the risk.

I close by speculating that long after Jesus concluded with His message, "blessed shall you be," and the crowd dispersed for home, Jesus's words of promise were not easily dismissed. The outcome of being transparent with yourself, and with God, is blessed shall you be.

> Showers of blessing, Showers of blessing we need: Mercy-drops round us are falling, But for the showers we plead. (Ezekiel 34:26–27)

Resources

Henry Matthew. Commentary on the Whole Bible: Complete Unabridged in One Volume.
Hendriksen, William. Baker New Testament Commentary: Matthew.
Blomberg, Craig L. The New American Commentary: Matthew.
Wiersbe, Warren W. The Bible Exposition Commentary.
Jamieson, Robert, Fausset, A. R, Brown, David. Commentary Critical and Explanatory on the Whole Bible.

CPSIA information can be obtained
at www.ICGtesting.com
Printed in the USA
LVHW090918080820
662689LV00003B/795